Find God

in

all things.

- St. Ignatius

This journal belongs to:

Name:_____

Email:_____

THE
examen
JOURNAL

FINDING GOD EVERY DAY

MARY WILLIAMS

2017

contents

OF THIS JOURNAL

what

IS THE EXAMEN?

In a nutshell, the Examen nurtures a lifestyle of coming to know God in the ordinary and extraordinary of our everyday. Founded by St. Ignatius of Loyola, the Examen is a method of personal daily prayer in which the individual reflects honestly on both the challenging and beautiful events of the past 24 hours. Men and women have used the Examen for hundreds of years as a means of discerning God's presence in their lives as well as how to live out their callings as unique human beings created to pour God's love out into the world.

The Examen is typically described in five parts:
1. Become aware of God's presence.
2. Express gratitude for your day.
3. Review the day honestly – the highs, the lows, and everything in between. Pay attention to your feelings as you remember specific moments.
4. Talk more deeply with God about a part of the day that is sticking with you. What would you say to God? What would God say to you?
5. Pray for tomorrow. Ask for the freedom to live your life more closely aligned with God.

Essentially, the Examen asks us to reflect upon moments of consolation (when we felt alive, energized, free, joy-filled) and moments of desolation (when we felt drained, anxious, trapped, angry). In the honest pondering of our daily highs and lows, we develop the beautiful habit of finding God in all things.

IS ST. IGNATIUS OF LOYOLA?

In 1521, a young Spanish soldier was struck in the leg by a cannonball during battle. He endured tremendous pain, multiple surgeries, and eventually amputation. His previous worldly life of military leadership was over. Bedridden, he became an avid reader. Because of a lack of books on other topics, he consumed book after book about Jesus and the saints. He soon fell in love with Jesus. It was during his long recovery, that St. Ignatius of Loyola (1491-1556) came to know Christ. He eventually went on to help found the Society of Jesus (the Jesuits). Hundreds of years later, he continues to transform the lives of women and men around the world. His personal journaling formed the foundation for his most famous book, *The Spiritual Exercises*, which included the Examen.

SHOULD I PRAY THE EXAMEN?

St. Ignatius actually intended for the members of his community to complete the Examen twice a day, once in the middle of the day and once at the end of the day. Since the Examen is an opportunity to reflect on the events of your day, sitting down in prayer with your journal sometime at the end of your day, when the past 24 hours are fresh in your mind, might be most beneficial. Dedicating a few minutes every single day after dinner or just before bed will help you create a life-long habit of daily reflection about where and how God is working in your everyday life. With that said, daily schedules are ever changing, and it is always more important to nurture the actual practice of spending time in prayer with God whenever that best happens during your day rather than to stress about missing a day. God's grace is always with us!

why and how

SHOULD I USE THIS JOURNAL?

The Examen Journal is inspired by Ignatian spirituality and created for those of us who appreciate regular journaling or would like to adopt a new spiritual practice.

Use this book heartily. We aren't perfect beings. Life is messy. Let the pages wrinkle with every entry. Let the binding crease with every quiet moment spent. Let the cover reflect your wildest adventures. The Examen Journal is meant to be well worn like that cozy blanket on your childhood bed or your favorite pair of running shoes or the tattered, yellowed edges of your grandmother's bible. Use it everyday. Write in it. Pray with it.

Think of the Examen Journal as a spiritual diary of sorts, a collection of your conversations with God, a history of the significant and simplest moments in your life that formed you into becoming the person that God so deeply wants you to be. Each entry is a love letter between you and God.

In this book, you will find 366 journal pages...one for each day of the year. If a day or a week or a few months are missed, simply continue where you left off. Don't stress. Life happens. God is always near.

Most importantly of all...

Just begin where you are.

And then in the words of St. Ignatius himself,
"Find God in all things."

Should you need some extra help, at the end of the journal you'll find a section titled, "Some Additional Guidance." Here you'll find the journal page unpacked a bit more...questions to ponder, thoughts about which to further reflect...almost a guided meditation.

THE *examen* JOURNAL

5 / 3 / 22

Thank you, God, for the gift of today. As I honestly review the events of the past 24 hours and pay attention to my feelings, I know your loving presence surrounds me. Bless my journal and our time spent together.

I felt alive in your presence today, God, when...

When Marinus talked with me and told me he wants to recommit to living out Your will for our relationship. You knew I needed to hear that and be convicted in that way, and Marinus was a ready conduit for Your grace. When we prayed together. In how he loves me and convicts me to love better.

I struggled to feel your presence today, God, when...

At work at times, and in the dark moments of weakness last night. It's strange that I almost think about You more in those moments that feel lost and desolate. I know I'm making a choice and I can hear You calling for me.

God, I want to share more deeply with you about one moment that stands out from today. Through this experience, I think you might be telling me...

In those moments where I know I'm not choosing You, I want to find a way to be convicted and redirected towards Your will — love & mercy itself. I feel like I'm always spinning out of control and I know I can find rest with You — grant me the grace to allow You to slow me down.

As I think about tomorrow, God, I pray that...

I pray for the grace to love better. Love You, love Marinus, love my family, my patients & coworkers. I know what You're calling me to — I pray for the grace to hear Your voice even more clearly and to respond in peace, without hesitation or resistance. I want to let You reign over every moment of my life. I love You, Lord God! Help me to love like You.

5 / 6 / 22

Thank you, God, for the gift of today. As I honestly review the events of the past 24 hours and pay attention to my feelings, I know your loving presence surrounds me. Bless my journal and our time spent together.

I felt alive in your presence today, God, when...

Praying at the end of the day. Scanning babies. Getting comps done. You love me so faithfully and I'm so grateful for all the ways You continue to bless me. Being with family.

I struggled to feel your presence today, God, when...

I got pretty wrapped up in clinic today, Lord. Help me to remember You. Give me perspective and remind me of Your call for my life. Don't let me get distracted by short-term, worldly goals and accomplishments. It's all for Your glory.

God, I want to share more deeply with you about one moment that stands out from today. Through this experience, I think you might be telling me...

I want my heart to be in communion with Yours. It's been so long, it almost took me by surprise. I want to be more in tune with You and the ways You're moving in my life. Help me to listen with my heart, be still & quiet, and allow You to move in me.

As I think about tomorrow, God, I pray that...

I remember to pray with Martinus. That I will bring Your love to everyone I encounter. That I will love my family & Martinus better, as You love them. That You would grant me the grace to draw closer to You. Thanksgiving.

5 / 11 / 22

Thank you, God, for the gift of today. As I honestly review the events of the past 24 hours and pay attention to my feelings, I know your loving presence surrounds me. Bless my journal and our time spent together.

I felt alive in your presence today, God, when...

I got to talk to Rachel, Marinus, and my mom.
When I found out I got good exam grades.
Praying a Rosary this morning

I struggled to feel your presence today, God, when...

At the end of the day talking to my mom (grace + patience). In class (distraction). Overwhelm. Anxiety.

God, I want to share more deeply with you about one moment that stands out from today. Through this experience, I think you might be telling me...

Help me to always remember that You are present with me, always ready to hold me up and carry me through. I forget too often to turn to You in moments of stress. Help me to be patient in this season, seek You out and look for the lesson You're trying to teach, and appreciate Your gift of the now.

As I think about tomorrow, God, I pray that...

to slow down, trust, rest, and listen. Guide my hands, feet, words, + heart to serve Your people and love the family You've trusted me with. I love You, God, and I pray to love You more each day. Help me to be patient and not to worry.

_____/_____/_____

Thank you, God, for the gift of today. As I honestly review the events of the past 24 hours and pay attention to my feelings, I know your loving presence surrounds me. Bless my journal and our time spent together.

I felt alive in your presence today, God, when...

I struggled to feel your presence today, God, when...

God, I want to share more deeply with you about one moment that stands out from today. Through this experience, I think you might be telling me...

As I think about tomorrow, God, I pray that...

_____ / _____ / _____

Thank you, God, for the gift of today. As I honestly review the events of the past 24 hours and pay attention to my feelings, I know your loving presence surrounds me. Bless my journal and our time spent together.

I felt alive in your presence today, God, when...   •

_____

_____

_____

_____

I struggled to feel your presence today, God, when...

_____

_____

_____

_____

God, I want to share more deeply with you about one moment that stands out from today. Through this experience, I think you might be telling me...

_____

_____

_____

_____

_____

As I think about tomorrow, God, I pray that...

_____

_____

_____

_____

_____

_____

_____

_____ / _____ / _____

Thank you, God, for the gift of today. As I honestly review the events of the past 24 hours and pay attention to my feelings, I know your loving presence surrounds me. Bless my journal and our time spent together.

I felt alive in your presence today, God, when...

_____

_____

_____

_____

I struggled to feel your presence today, God, when...

_____

_____

_____

_____

God, I want to share more deeply with you about one moment that stands out from today. Through this experience, I think you might be telling me...

_____

_____

_____

_____

_____

As I think about tomorrow, God, I pray that...

_____

_____

_____

_____

_____

_____

_____ / _____ / _____

Thank you, God, for the gift of today. As I honestly review the events of the past 24 hours and pay attention to my feelings, I know your loving presence surrounds me. Bless my journal and our time spent together.

I felt alive in your presence today, God, when...

_____

_____

_____

_____

I struggled to feel your presence today, God, when...

_____

_____

_____

_____

God, I want to share more deeply with you about one moment that stands out from today. Through this experience, I think you might be telling me...

_____

_____

_____

_____

_____

As I think about tomorrow, God, I pray that...

_____

_____

_____

_____

_____

_____

Thank you, God, for the gift of today. As I honestly review the events of the past 24 hours and pay attention to my feelings, I know your loving presence surrounds me. Bless my journal and our time spent together.

I felt alive in your presence today, God, when…

_____

_____

_____

_____

I struggled to feel your presence today, God, when…

_____

_____

_____

_____

God, I want to share more deeply with you about one moment that stands out from today. Through this experience, I think you might be telling me…

_____

_____

_____

_____

_____

As I think about tomorrow, God, I pray that…

_____

_____

_____

_____

_____

_____

_____ / _____ / _____

Thank you, God, for the gift of today. As I honestly review the events of the past 24 hours and pay attention to my feelings, I know your loving presence surrounds me. Bless my journal and our time spent together.

I felt alive in your presence today, God, when...

_____

_____

_____

_____

I struggled to feel your presence today, God, when...

_____

_____

_____

_____

God, I want to share more deeply with you about one moment that stands out from today. Through this experience, I think you might be telling me...

_____

_____

_____

_____

As I think about tomorrow, God, I pray that...

_____

_____

_____

_____

_____

_____

Thank you, God, for the gift of today. As I honestly review the events of the past 24 hours and pay attention to my feelings, I know your loving presence surrounds me. Bless my journal and our time spent together.

I felt alive in your presence today, God, when...

_____

_____

_____

_____

_____

I struggled to feel your presence today, God, when...

_____

_____

_____

_____

God, I want to share more deeply with you about one moment that stands out from today. Through this experience, I think you might be telling me...

_____

_____

_____

_____

_____

As I think about tomorrow, God, I pray that...

_____

_____

_____

_____

_____

_____

_____

Thank you, God, for the gift of today. As I honestly review the events of the past 24 hours and pay attention to my feelings, I know your loving presence surrounds me. Bless my journal and our time spent together.

I felt alive in your presence today, God, when...

_____

_____

_____

_____

I struggled to feel your presence today, God, when...

_____

_____

_____

_____

God, I want to share more deeply with you about one moment that stands out from today. Through this experience, I think you might be telling me...

_____

_____

_____

_____

_____

As I think about tomorrow, God, I pray that...

_____

_____

_____

_____

_____

_____

_____ / _____ /

Thank you, God, for the gift of today. As I honestly review the events of the past 24 hours and pay attention to my feelings, I know your loving presence surrounds me. Bless my journal and our time spent together.

I felt alive in your presence today, God, when...

_____

_____

_____

_____

_____

I struggled to feel your presence today, God, when...

_____

_____

_____

_____

_____

God, I want to share more deeply with you about one moment that stands out from today. Through this experience, I think you might be telling me...

_____

_____

_____

_____

_____

As I think about tomorrow, God, I pray that...

_____

_____

_____

_____

_____

_____

_____ / _____ / _____

Thank you, God, for the gift of today. As I honestly review the events of the past 24 hours and pay attention to my feelings, I know your loving presence surrounds me. Bless my journal and our time spent together.

I felt alive in your presence today, God, when...

_____

_____

_____

_____

I struggled to feel your presence today, God, when...

_____

_____

_____

_____

God, I want to share more deeply with you about one moment that stands out from today. Through this experience, I think you might be telling me...

_____

_____

_____

_____

As I think about tomorrow, God, I pray that...

_____

_____

_____

_____

_____

_____

_____ / _____ / _____

Thank you, God, for the gift of today. As I honestly review the events of the past 24 hours and pay attention to my feelings, I know your loving presence surrounds me. Bless my journal and our time spent together.

I felt alive in your presence today, God, when...

_____

_____

_____

_____

I struggled to feel your presence today, God, when...

_____

_____

_____

_____

God, I want to share more deeply with you about one moment that stands out from today. Through this experience, I think you might be telling me...

_____

_____

_____

_____

_____

As I think about tomorrow, God, I pray that...

_____

_____

_____

_____

_____

_____

_____ / _____ / _____

Thank you, God, for the gift of today. As I honestly review the events of the past 24 hours and pay attention to my feelings, I know your loving presence surrounds me. Bless my journal and our time spent together.

I felt alive in your presence today, God, when...

_____

_____

_____

_____

_____

I struggled to feel your presence today, God, when...

_____

_____

_____

_____

God, I want to share more deeply with you about one moment that stands out from today. Through this experience, I think you might be telling me...

_____

_____

_____

_____

_____

As I think about tomorrow, God, I pray that...

_____

_____

_____

_____

_____

_____

_____ / _____ / _____

Thank you, God, for the gift of today. As I honestly review the events of the past 24 hours and pay attention to my feelings, I know your loving presence surrounds me. Bless my journal and our time spent together.

I felt alive in your presence today, God, when...

_____
_____
_____
_____
_____

I struggled to feel your presence today, God, when...

_____
_____
_____
_____

God, I want to share more deeply with you about one moment that stands out from today. Through this experience, I think you might be telling me...

_____
_____
_____
_____
_____

As I think about tomorrow, God, I pray that...

_____
_____
_____
_____
_____
_____

_____ / _____ / _____

Thank you, God, for the gift of today. As I honestly review the events of the past 24 hours and pay attention to my feelings, I know your loving presence surrounds me. Bless my journal and our time spent together.

I felt alive in your presence today, God, when...

_____

_____

_____

_____

I struggled to feel your presence today, God, when...

_____

_____

_____

_____

God, I want to share more deeply with you about one moment that stands out from today. Through this experience, I think you might be telling me...

_____

_____

_____

_____

_____

As I think about tomorrow, God, I pray that...

_____

_____

_____

_____

_____

_____

_____/_____/_____

Thank you, God, for the gift of today. As I honestly review the events of the past 24 hours and pay attention to my feelings, I know your loving presence surrounds me. Bless my journal and our time spent together.

I felt alive in your presence today, God, when...

I struggled to feel your presence today, God, when...

God, I want to share more deeply with you about one moment that stands out from today. Through this experience, I think you might be telling me...

As I think about tomorrow, God, I pray that...

_____ / _____ / _____

Thank you, God, for the gift of today. As I honestly review the events of the past 24 hours and pay attention to my feelings, I know your loving presence surrounds me. Bless my journal and our time spent together.

I felt alive in your presence today, God, when...

_____

_____

_____

_____

I struggled to feel your presence today, God, when...

_____

_____

_____

_____

God, I want to share more deeply with you about one moment that stands out from today. Through this experience, I think you might be telling me...

_____

_____

_____

_____

_____

As I think about tomorrow, God, I pray that...

_____

_____

_____

_____

_____

_____

Thank you, God, for the gift of today. As I honestly review the events of the past 24 hours and pay attention to my feelings, I know your loving presence surrounds me. Bless my journal and our time spent together.

I felt alive in your presence today, God, when...

_____
_____
_____
_____
_____

I struggled to feel your presence today, God, when...

_____
_____
_____
_____

God, I want to share more deeply with you about one moment that stands out from today. Through this experience, I think you might be telling me...

_____
_____
_____
_____
_____

As I think about tomorrow, God, I pray that...

_____
_____
_____
_____
_____
_____

_____ / _____ / _____

Thank you, God, for the gift of today. As I honestly review the events of the past 24 hours and pay attention to my feelings, I know your loving presence surrounds me. Bless my journal and our time spent together.

I felt alive in your presence today, God, when...

_____

_____

_____

_____

_____

I struggled to feel your presence today, God, when...

_____

_____

_____

_____

God, I want to share more deeply with you about one moment that stands out from today. Through this experience, I think you might be telling me...

_____

_____

_____

_____

_____

As I think about tomorrow, God, I pray that...

_____

_____

_____

_____

_____

_____

_____

Thank you, God, for the gift of today. As I honestly review the events of the past 24 hours and pay attention to my feelings, I know your loving presence surrounds me. Bless my journal and our time spent together.

I felt alive in your presence today, God, when...

_____

_____

_____

_____

I struggled to feel your presence today, God, when...

_____

_____

_____

_____

God, I want to share more deeply with you about one moment that stands out from today. Through this experience, I think you might be telling me...

_____

_____

_____

_____

_____

As I think about tomorrow, God, I pray that...

_____

_____

_____

_____

_____

_____

_____ / _____ / _____

Thank you, God, for the gift of today. As I honestly review the events of the past 24 hours and pay attention to my feelings, I know your loving presence surrounds me. Bless my journal and our time spent together.

I felt alive in your presence today, God, when...

_____
_____
_____
_____

I struggled to feel your presence today, God, when...

_____
_____
_____
_____

God, I want to share more deeply with you about one moment that stands out from today. Through this experience, I think you might be telling me...

_____
_____
_____
_____

As I think about tomorrow, God, I pray that...

_____
_____
_____
_____
_____
_____

Thank you, God, for the gift of today. As I honestly review the events of the past 24 hours and pay attention to my feelings, I know your loving presence surrounds me. Bless my journal and our time spent together.

I felt alive in your presence today, God, when...

I struggled to feel your presence today, God, when...

God, I want to share more deeply with you about one moment that stands out from today. Through this experience, I think you might be telling me...

As I think about tomorrow, God, I pray that...

_____ / _____ / _____

Thank you, God, for the gift of today. As I honestly review the events of the past 24 hours and pay attention to my feelings, I know your loving presence surrounds me. Bless my journal and our time spent together.

I felt alive in your presence today, God, when...

_____

_____

_____

_____

_____

I struggled to feel your presence today, God, when...

_____

_____

_____

_____

_____

God, I want to share more deeply with you about one moment that stands out from today. Through this experience, I think you might be telling me...

_____

_____

_____

_____

_____

_____

As I think about tomorrow, God, I pray that...

_____

_____

_____

_____

_____

_____

_____

_____ / _____ /

Thank you, God, for the gift of today. As I honestly review the events of the past 24 hours and pay attention to my feelings, I know your loving presence surrounds me. Bless my journal and our time spent together.

I felt alive in your presence today, God, when...

_____
_____
_____
_____
_____

I struggled to feel your presence today, God, when...

_____
_____
_____
_____

God, I want to share more deeply with you about one moment that stands out from today. Through this experience, I think you might be telling me...

_____
_____
_____
_____
_____

As I think about tomorrow, God, I pray that...

_____
_____
_____
_____
_____
_____

Thank you, God, for the gift of today. As I honestly review the events of the past 24 hours and pay attention to my feelings, I know your loving presence surrounds me. Bless my journal and our time spent together.

I felt alive in your presence today, God, when...

I struggled to feel your presence today, God, when...

God, I want to share more deeply with you about one moment that stands out from today. Through this experience, I think you might be telling me...

As I think about tomorrow, God, I pray that...

_____ / _____ / _____

Thank you, God, for the gift of today. As I honestly review the events of the past 24 hours and pay attention to my feelings, I know your loving presence surrounds me. Bless my journal and our time spent together.

I felt alive in your presence today, God, when...

_____
_____
_____
_____
_____

I struggled to feel your presence today, God, when...

_____
_____
_____
_____
_____

God, I want to share more deeply with you about one moment that stands out from today. Through this experience, I think you might be telling me...

_____
_____
_____
_____
_____
_____

As I think about tomorrow, God, I pray that...

_____
_____
_____
_____
_____
_____
_____

Thank you, God, for the gift of today. As I honestly review the events of the past 24 hours and pay attention to my feelings, I know your loving presence surrounds me. Bless my journal and our time spent together.

I felt alive in your presence today, God, when...

I struggled to feel your presence today, God, when...

God, I want to share more deeply with you about one moment that stands out from today. Through this experience, I think you might be telling me...

As I think about tomorrow, God, I pray that...

_____ / _____ /

Thank you, God, for the gift of today. As I honestly review the events of the past 24 hours and pay attention to my feelings, I know your loving presence surrounds me. Bless my journal and our time spent together.

I felt alive in your presence today, God, when...

_____

_____

_____

_____

I struggled to feel your presence today, God, when...

_____

_____

_____

_____

God, I want to share more deeply with you about one moment that stands out from today. Through this experience, I think you might be telling me...

_____

_____

_____

_____

_____

As I think about tomorrow, God, I pray that...

_____

_____

_____

_____

_____

_____

_____/_____/_____

Thank you, God, for the gift of today. As I honestly review the events of the past 24 hours and pay attention to my feelings, I know your loving presence surrounds me. Bless my journal and our time spent together.

I felt alive in your presence today, God, when...

_____

_____

_____

_____

I struggled to feel your presence today, God, when...

_____

_____

_____

_____

God, I want to share more deeply with you about one moment that stands out from today. Through this experience, I think you might be telling me...

_____

_____

_____

_____

_____

As I think about tomorrow, God, I pray that...

_____

_____

_____

_____

_____

_____

_____ / _____ /

Thank you, God, for the gift of today. As I honestly review the events of the past 24 hours and pay attention to my feelings, I know your loving presence surrounds me. Bless my journal and our time spent together.

I felt alive in your presence today, God, when...

_____

_____

_____

_____

_____

I struggled to feel your presence today, God, when...

_____

_____

_____

_____

God, I want to share more deeply with you about one moment that stands out from today. Through this experience, I think you might be telling me...

_____

_____

_____

_____

_____

As I think about tomorrow, God, I pray that...

_____

_____

_____

_____

_____

_____

Soul of Christ,
sanctify me.

Body of Christ,
save me.

Blood of Christ,
inebriate me.

Water from the side of Christ,
wash me.

Passion of Christ,
strengthen me.

Good Jesus,
hear me.

Within the wounds,
shelter me.

From turning away,
keep me.

From the evil one,
protect me.

At the hour of my death,
call me.

Into your presence *lead me*
to praise you with all your saints.
Forever and ever

Amen.

- St. Ignatius

_____ / _____ / _____

Thank you, God, for the gift of today. As I honestly review the events of the past 24 hours and pay attention to my feelings, I know your loving presence surrounds me. Bless my journal and our time spent together.

I felt alive in your presence today, God, when...

I struggled to feel your presence today, God, when...

God, I want to share more deeply with you about one moment that stands out from today. Through this experience, I think you might be telling me...

As I think about tomorrow, God, I pray that...

_____ / _____ / _____

Thank you, God, for the gift of today. As I honestly review the events of the past 24 hours and pay attention to my feelings, I know your loving presence surrounds me. Bless my journal and our time spent together.

I felt alive in your presence today, God, when...

_____

_____

_____

_____

I struggled to feel your presence today, God, when...

_____

_____

_____

God, I want to share more deeply with you about one moment that stands out from today. Through this experience, I think you might be telling me...

_____

_____

_____

_____

As I think about tomorrow, God, I pray that...

_____

_____

_____

_____

_____

_____

_____ / _____ / _____

Thank you, God, for the gift of today. As I honestly review the events of the past 24 hours and pay attention to my feelings, I know your loving presence surrounds me. Bless my journal and our time spent together.

I felt alive in your presence today, God, when...

_____

_____

_____

_____

I struggled to feel your presence today, God, when...

_____

_____

_____

_____

God, I want to share more deeply with you about one moment that stands out from today. Through this experience, I think you might be telling me...

_____

_____

_____

_____

_____

As I think about tomorrow, God, I pray that...

_____

_____

_____

_____

_____

_____

_____ / _____ / _____

Thank you, God, for the gift of today. As I honestly review the events of the past 24 hours and pay attention to my feelings, I know your loving presence surrounds me. Bless my journal and our time spent together.

I felt alive in your presence today, God, when...

_____

_____

_____

_____

I struggled to feel your presence today, God, when...

_____

_____

_____

_____

God, I want to share more deeply with you about one moment that stands out from today. Through this experience, I think you might be telling me...

_____

_____

_____

_____

_____

As I think about tomorrow, God, I pray that...

_____

_____

_____

_____

_____

_____

_____ / _____ / _____

Thank you, God, for the gift of today. As I honestly review the events of the past 24 hours and pay attention to my feelings, I know your loving presence surrounds me. Bless my journal and our time spent together.

I felt alive in your presence today, God, when...

_____

_____

_____

_____

I struggled to feel your presence today, God, when...

_____

_____

_____

_____

God, I want to share more deeply with you about one moment that stands out from today. Through this experience, I think you might be telling me...

_____

_____

_____

_____

_____

As I think about tomorrow, God, I pray that...

_____

_____

_____

_____

_____

_____

_____ / _____ / _____

Thank you, God, for the gift of today. As I honestly review the events of the past 24 hours and pay attention to my feelings, I know your loving presence surrounds me. Bless my journal and our time spent together.

I felt alive in your presence today, God, when...

I struggled to feel your presence today, God, when...

God, I want to share more deeply with you about one moment that stands out from today. Through this experience, I think you might be telling me...

As I think about tomorrow, God, I pray that...

_____ / _____ /

Thank you, God, for the gift of today. As I honestly review the events of the past 24 hours and pay attention to my feelings, I know your loving presence surrounds me. Bless my journal and our time spent together.

I felt alive in your presence today, God, when...

_____

_____

_____

_____

_____

I struggled to feel your presence today, God, when...

_____

_____

_____

_____

God, I want to share more deeply with you about one moment that stands out from today. Through this experience, I think you might be telling me...

_____

_____

_____

_____

_____

As I think about tomorrow, God, I pray that...

_____

_____

_____

_____

_____

_____

_____/_____/_____

Thank you, God, for the gift of today. As I honestly review the events of the past 24 hours and pay attention to my feelings, I know your loving presence surrounds me. Bless my journal and our time spent together.

I felt alive in your presence today, God, when...

_____

_____

_____

_____

I struggled to feel your presence today, God, when...

_____

_____

_____

_____

God, I want to share more deeply with you about one moment that stands out from today. Through this experience, I think you might be telling me...

_____

_____

_____

_____

_____

As I think about tomorrow, God, I pray that...

_____

_____

_____

_____

_____

_____

_____ / _____ / _____

Thank you, God, for the gift of today. As I honestly review the events of the past 24 hours and pay attention to my feelings, I know your loving presence surrounds me. Bless my journal and our time spent together.

I felt alive in your presence today, God, when...

_____

_____

_____

_____

I struggled to feel your presence today, God, when...

_____

_____

_____

_____

God, I want to share more deeply with you about one moment that stands out from today. Through this experience, I think you might be telling me...

_____

_____

_____

_____

_____

As I think about tomorrow, God, I pray that...

_____

_____

_____

_____

_____

_____

_____ / _____ / _____

Thank you, God, for the gift of today. As I honestly review the events of the past 24 hours and pay attention to my feelings, I know your loving presence surrounds me. Bless my journal and our time spent together.

I felt alive in your presence today, God, when...

_____

_____

_____

_____

_____

I struggled to feel your presence today, God, when...

_____

_____

_____

_____

_____

God, I want to share more deeply with you about one moment that stands out from today. Through this experience, I think you might be telling me...

_____

_____

_____

_____

_____

As I think about tomorrow, God, I pray that...

_____

_____

_____

_____

_____

_____

_____

_____ / _____ / _____

Thank you, God, for the gift of today. As I honestly review the events of the past 24 hours and pay attention to my feelings, I know your loving presence surrounds me. Bless my journal and our time spent together.

I felt alive in your presence today, God, when...

_____

_____

_____

_____

_____

I struggled to feel your presence today, God, when...

_____

_____

_____

_____

_____

God, I want to share more deeply with you about one moment that stands out from today. Through this experience, I think you might be telling me...

_____

_____

_____

_____

_____

_____

As I think about tomorrow, God, I pray that...

_____

_____

_____

_____

_____

_____

_____

_____ / _____ / _____

Thank you, God, for the gift of today. As I honestly review the events of the past 24 hours and pay attention to my feelings, I know your loving presence surrounds me. Bless my journal and our time spent together.

I felt alive in your presence today, God, when...

I struggled to feel your presence today, God, when...

God, I want to share more deeply with you about one moment that stands out from today. Through this experience, I think you might be telling me...

As I think about tomorrow, God, I pray that...

_____ / _____ / _____

Thank you, God, for the gift of today. As I honestly review the events of the past 24 hours and pay attention to my feelings, I know your loving presence surrounds me. Bless my journal and our time spent together.

I felt alive in your presence today, God, when...

_____

_____

_____

_____

I struggled to feel your presence today, God, when...

_____

_____

_____

_____

God, I want to share more deeply with you about one moment that stands out from today. Through this experience, I think you might be telling me...

_____

_____

_____

_____

_____

As I think about tomorrow, God, I pray that...

_____

_____

_____

_____

_____

_____

Thank you, God, for the gift of today. As I honestly review the events of the past 24 hours and pay attention to my feelings, I know your loving presence surrounds me. Bless my journal and our time spent together.

I felt alive in your presence today, God, when...

I struggled to feel your presence today, God, when...

God, I want to share more deeply with you about one moment that stands out from today. Through this experience, I think you might be telling me...

As I think about tomorrow, God, I pray that...

_____ / _____ /

Thank you, God, for the gift of today. As I honestly review the events of the past 24 hours and pay attention to my feelings, I know your loving presence surrounds me. Bless my journal and our time spent together.

I felt alive in your presence today, God, when...

_____
_____
_____
_____
_____

I struggled to feel your presence today, God, when...

_____
_____
_____
_____

God, I want to share more deeply with you about one moment that stands out from today. Through this experience, I think you might be telling me...

_____
_____
_____
_____
_____

As I think about tomorrow, God, I pray that...

_____
_____
_____
_____
_____
_____

_____ / _____ / _____

Thank you, God, for the gift of today. As I honestly review the events of the past 24 hours and pay attention to my feelings, I know your loving presence surrounds me. Bless my journal and our time spent together.

I felt alive in your presence today, God, when...

_____
_____
_____
_____

I struggled to feel your presence today, God, when...

_____
_____
_____

God, I want to share more deeply with you about one moment that stands out from today. Through this experience, I think you might be telling me...

_____
_____
_____
_____

As I think about tomorrow, God, I pray that...

_____
_____
_____
_____
_____
_____

_____ / _____ / _____

Thank you, God, for the gift of today. As I honestly review the events of the past 24 hours and pay attention to my feelings, I know your loving presence surrounds me. Bless my journal and our time spent together.

I felt alive in your presence today, God, when...

_____

_____

_____

_____

_____

I struggled to feel your presence today, God, when...

_____

_____

_____

_____

God, I want to share more deeply with you about one moment that stands out from today. Through this experience, I think you might be telling me...

_____

_____

_____

_____

_____

As I think about tomorrow, God, I pray that...

_____

_____

_____

_____

_____

_____

_____ / _____ / _____

Thank you, God, for the gift of today. As I honestly review the events of the past 24 hours and pay attention to my feelings, I know your loving presence surrounds me. Bless my journal and our time spent together.

I felt alive in your presence today, God, when...

_____

_____

_____

_____

I struggled to feel your presence today, God, when...

_____

_____

_____

_____

God, I want to share more deeply with you about one moment that stands out from today. Through this experience, I think you might be telling me...

_____

_____

_____

_____

_____

As I think about tomorrow, God, I pray that...

_____

_____

_____

_____

_____

_____

Thank you, God, for the gift of today. As I honestly review the events of the past 24 hours and pay attention to my feelings, I know your loving presence surrounds me. Bless my journal and our time spent together.

I felt alive in your presence today, God, when...

_____

_____

_____

_____

I struggled to feel your presence today, God, when...

_____

_____

_____

God, I want to share more deeply with you about one moment that stands out from today. Through this experience, I think you might be telling me...

_____

_____

_____

_____

As I think about tomorrow, God, I pray that...

_____

_____

_____

_____

_____

_____

_____ / _____ / _____

Thank you, God, for the gift of today. As I honestly review the events of the past 24 hours and pay attention to my feelings, I know your loving presence surrounds me. Bless my journal and our time spent together.

I felt alive in your presence today, God, when...

_____

_____

_____

_____

_____

I struggled to feel your presence today, God, when...

_____

_____

_____

_____

_____

God, I want to share more deeply with you about one moment that stands out from today. Through this experience, I think you might be telling me...

_____

_____

_____

_____

_____

As I think about tomorrow, God, I pray that...

_____

_____

_____

_____

_____

_____

_____

_____ / _____ / _____

Thank you, God, for the gift of today. As I honestly review the events of the past 24 hours and pay attention to my feelings, I know your loving presence surrounds me. Bless my journal and our time spent together.

I felt alive in your presence today, God, when...

_____

_____

_____

_____

I struggled to feel your presence today, God, when...

_____

_____

_____

_____

God, I want to share more deeply with you about one moment that stands out from today. Through this experience, I think you might be telling me...

_____

_____

_____

_____

_____

As I think about tomorrow, God, I pray that...

_____

_____

_____

_____

_____

_____

Thank you, God, for the gift of today. As I honestly review the events of the past 24 hours and pay attention to my feelings, I know your loving presence surrounds me. Bless my journal and our time spent together.

I felt alive in your presence today, God, when...

_____

_____

_____

_____

I struggled to feel your presence today, God, when...

_____

_____

_____

_____

God, I want to share more deeply with you about one moment that stands out from today. Through this experience, I think you might be telling me...

_____

_____

_____

_____

_____

As I think about tomorrow, God, I pray that...

_____

_____

_____

_____

_____

_____

Thank you, God, for the gift of today. As I honestly review the events of the past 24 hours and pay attention to my feelings, I know your loving presence surrounds me. Bless my journal and our time spent together.

I felt alive in your presence today, God, when...

_____

_____

_____

_____

_____

I struggled to feel your presence today, God, when...

_____

_____

_____

_____

God, I want to share more deeply with you about one moment that stands out from today. Through this experience, I think you might be telling me...

_____

_____

_____

_____

_____

As I think about tomorrow, God, I pray that...

_____

_____

_____

_____

_____

_____

Thank you, God, for the gift of today. As I honestly review the events of the past 24 hours and pay attention to my feelings, I know your loving presence surrounds me. Bless my journal and our time spent together.

I felt alive in your presence today, God, when...

_____

_____

_____

_____

I struggled to feel your presence today, God, when...

_____

_____

_____

_____

God, I want to share more deeply with you about one moment that stands out from today. Through this experience, I think you might be telling me...

_____

_____

_____

_____

_____

As I think about tomorrow, God, I pray that...

_____

_____

_____

_____

_____

_____

_____

_____/_____/_____

Thank you, God, for the gift of today. As I honestly review the events of the past 24 hours and pay attention to my feelings, I know your loving presence surrounds me. Bless my journal and our time spent together.

I felt alive in your presence today, God, when...

_____
_____
_____
_____
_____

I struggled to feel your presence today, God, when...

_____
_____
_____
_____
_____

God, I want to share more deeply with you about one moment that stands out from today. Through this experience, I think you might be telling me...

_____
_____
_____
_____
_____

As I think about tomorrow, God, I pray that...

_____
_____
_____
_____
_____
_____
_____

_____ / _____ / _____

Thank you, God, for the gift of today. As I honestly review the events of the past 24 hours and pay attention to my feelings, I know your loving presence surrounds me. Bless my journal and our time spent together.

I felt alive in your presence today, God, when...

_____

_____

_____

_____

I struggled to feel your presence today, God, when...

_____

_____

_____

_____

God, I want to share more deeply with you about one moment that stands out from today. Through this experience, I think you might be telling me...

_____

_____

_____

_____

As I think about tomorrow, God, I pray that...

_____

_____

_____

_____

_____

_____

_____/_____/_____

Thank you, God, for the gift of today. As I honestly review the events of the past 24 hours and pay attention to my feelings, I know your loving presence surrounds me. Bless my journal and our time spent together.

I felt alive in your presence today, God, when...

_____

_____

_____

_____

I struggled to feel your presence today, God, when...

_____

_____

_____

_____

God, I want to share more deeply with you about one moment that stands out from today. Through this experience, I think you might be telling me...

_____

_____

_____

_____

_____

As I think about tomorrow, God, I pray that...

_____

_____

_____

_____

_____

_____

_____/_____/_____

Thank you, God, for the gift of today. As I honestly review the events of the past 24 hours and pay attention to my feelings, I know your loving presence surrounds me. Bless my journal and our time spent together.

I felt alive in your presence today, God, when...

_____

_____

_____

_____

I struggled to feel your presence today, God, when...

_____

_____

_____

_____

God, I want to share more deeply with you about one moment that stands out from today. Through this experience, I think you might be telling me...

_____

_____

_____

_____

_____

As I think about tomorrow, God, I pray that...

_____

_____

_____

_____

_____

_____

_____

_____ / _____ / _____

Thank you, God, for the gift of today. As I honestly review the events of the past 24 hours and pay attention to my feelings, I know your loving presence surrounds me. Bless my journal and our time spent together.

I felt alive in your presence today, God, when...

_____

_____

_____

_____

I struggled to feel your presence today, God, when...

_____

_____

_____

God, I want to share more deeply with you about one moment that stands out from today. Through this experience, I think you might be telling me...

_____

_____

_____

_____

As I think about tomorrow, God, I pray that...

_____

_____

_____

_____

_____

_____/_____/_____

Thank you, God, for the gift of today. As I honestly review the events of the past 24 hours and pay attention to my feelings, I know your loving presence surrounds me. Bless my journal and our time spent together.

I felt alive in your presence today, God, when...

_____

_____

_____

_____

_____

I struggled to feel your presence today, God, when...

_____

_____

_____

_____

God, I want to share more deeply with you about one moment that stands out from today. Through this experience, I think you might be telling me...

_____

_____

_____

_____

_____

As I think about tomorrow, God, I pray that...

_____

_____

_____

_____

_____

_____

_____

_____ / _____ / _____

Thank you, God, for the gift of today. As I honestly review the events of the past 24 hours and pay attention to my feelings, I know your loving presence surrounds me. Bless my journal and our time spent together.

I felt alive in your presence today, God, when...

_____

_____

_____

_____

_____

I struggled to feel your presence today, God, when...

_____

_____

_____

_____

God, I want to share more deeply with you about one moment that stands out from today. Through this experience, I think you might be telling me...

_____

_____

_____

_____

_____

As I think about tomorrow, God, I pray that...

_____

_____

_____

_____

_____

_____

ACT AS IF EVERYTHING
DEPENDED ON YOU;
TRUST AS IF EVERYTHING
DEPENDED ON GOD.

- St. Ignatius

_____/_____/_____

Thank you, God, for the gift of today. As I honestly review the events of the past 24 hours and pay attention to my feelings, I know your loving presence surrounds me. Bless my journal and our time spent together.

I felt alive in your presence today, God, when...

_____
_____
_____
_____

I struggled to feel your presence today, God, when...

_____
_____
_____
_____

God, I want to share more deeply with you about one moment that stands out from today. Through this experience, I think you might be telling me...

_____
_____
_____
_____
_____

As I think about tomorrow, God, I pray that...

_____
_____
_____
_____
_____
_____

_____ / _____ / _____

Thank you, God, for the gift of today. As I honestly review the events of the past 24 hours and pay attention to my feelings, I know your loving presence surrounds me. Bless my journal and our time spent together.

I felt alive in your presence today, God, when...

_____

_____

_____

_____

I struggled to feel your presence today, God, when...

_____

_____

_____

_____

God, I want to share more deeply with you about one moment that stands out from today. Through this experience, I think you might be telling me...

_____

_____

_____

_____

As I think about tomorrow, God, I pray that...

_____

_____

_____

_____

_____

_____

_____ / _____ / _____

Thank you, God, for the gift of today. As I honestly review the events of the past 24 hours and pay attention to my feelings, I know your loving presence surrounds me. Bless my journal and our time spent together.

I felt alive in your presence today, God, when...

_____

_____

_____

_____

_____

I struggled to feel your presence today, God, when...

_____

_____

_____

_____

God, I want to share more deeply with you about one moment that stands out from today. Through this experience, I think you might be telling me...

_____

_____

_____

_____

_____

As I think about tomorrow, God, I pray that...

_____

_____

_____

_____

_____

_____

_____/_____/_____

Thank you, God, for the gift of today. As I honestly review the events of the past 24 hours and pay attention to my feelings, I know your loving presence surrounds me. Bless my journal and our time spent together.

I felt alive in your presence today, God, when...

_____

_____

_____

_____

I struggled to feel your presence today, God, when...

_____

_____

_____

God, I want to share more deeply with you about one moment that stands out from today. Through this experience, I think you might be telling me...

_____

_____

_____

_____

As I think about tomorrow, God, I pray that...

_____

_____

_____

_____

_____

_____

_____ / _____ / _____

Thank you, God, for the gift of today. As I honestly review the events of the past 24 hours and pay attention to my feelings, I know your loving presence surrounds me. Bless my journal and our time spent together.

I felt alive in your presence today, God, when...

_____

_____

_____

_____

_____

I struggled to feel your presence today, God, when...

_____

_____

_____

_____

God, I want to share more deeply with you about one moment that stands out from today. Through this experience, I think you might be telling me...

_____

_____

_____

_____

_____

As I think about tomorrow, God, I pray that...

_____

_____

_____

_____

_____

_____

_____ / _____ / _____

Thank you, God, for the gift of today. As I honestly review the events of the past 24 hours and pay attention to my feelings, I know your loving presence surrounds me. Bless my journal and our time spent together.

I felt alive in your presence today, God, when...

_____

_____

_____

_____

I struggled to feel your presence today, God, when...

_____

_____

_____

_____

God, I want to share more deeply with you about one moment that stands out from today. Through this experience, I think you might be telling me...

_____

_____

_____

_____

As I think about tomorrow, God, I pray that...

_____

_____

_____

_____

_____

_____

_____ / _____ / _____

Thank you, God, for the gift of today. As I honestly review the events of the past 24 hours and pay attention to my feelings, I know your loving presence surrounds me. Bless my journal and our time spent together.

I felt alive in your presence today, God, when...

_____

_____

_____

_____

I struggled to feel your presence today, God, when...

_____

_____

_____

_____

God, I want to share more deeply with you about one moment that stands out from today. Through this experience, I think you might be telling me...

_____

_____

_____

_____

_____

As I think about tomorrow, God, I pray that...

_____

_____

_____

_____

_____

_____

_____ / _____ / _____

Thank you, God, for the gift of today. As I honestly review the events of the past 24 hours and pay attention to my feelings, I know your loving presence surrounds me. Bless my journal and our time spent together.

I felt alive in your presence today, God, when...

_____

_____

_____

_____

I struggled to feel your presence today, God, when...

_____

_____

_____

God, I want to share more deeply with you about one moment that stands out from today. Through this experience, I think you might be telling me...

_____

_____

_____

_____

As I think about tomorrow, God, I pray that...

_____

_____

_____

_____

_____

_____

_____ / _____ /

Thank you, God, for the gift of today. As I honestly review the events of the past 24 hours and pay attention to my feelings, I know your loving presence surrounds me. Bless my journal and our time spent together.

I felt alive in your presence today, God, when...

_____

_____

_____

_____

_____

I struggled to feel your presence today, God, when...

_____

_____

_____

_____

God, I want to share more deeply with you about one moment that stands out from today. Through this experience, I think you might be telling me...

_____

_____

_____

_____

_____

As I think about tomorrow, God, I pray that...

_____

_____

_____

_____

_____

_____

_____ / _____ / _____

Thank you, God, for the gift of today. As I honestly review the events of the past 24 hours and pay attention to my feelings, I know your loving presence surrounds me. Bless my journal and our time spent together.

I felt alive in your presence today, God, when...

_____
_____
_____
_____
_____

I struggled to feel your presence today, God, when...

_____
_____
_____
_____

God, I want to share more deeply with you about one moment that stands out from today. Through this experience, I think you might be telling me...

_____
_____
_____
_____
_____

As I think about tomorrow, God, I pray that...

_____
_____
_____
_____
_____
_____

_____ / _____ / _____

Thank you, God, for the gift of today. As I honestly review the events of the past 24 hours and pay attention to my feelings, I know your loving presence surrounds me. Bless my journal and our time spent together.

I felt alive in your presence today, God, when...

_____

_____

_____

_____

_____

I struggled to feel your presence today, God, when...

_____

_____

_____

_____

God, I want to share more deeply with you about one moment that stands out from today. Through this experience, I think you might be telling me...

_____

_____

_____

_____

_____

As I think about tomorrow, God, I pray that...

_____

_____

_____

_____

_____

_____

_____

_____ / _____ / _____

Thank you, God, for the gift of today. As I honestly review the events of the past 24 hours and pay attention to my feelings, I know your loving presence surrounds me. Bless my journal and our time spent together.

I felt alive in your presence today, God, when...

_____

_____

_____

_____

I struggled to feel your presence today, God, when...

_____

_____

_____

_____

God, I want to share more deeply with you about one moment that stands out from today. Through this experience, I think you might be telling me...

_____

_____

_____

_____

_____

As I think about tomorrow, God, I pray that...

_____

_____

_____

_____

_____

_____

_____ / _____ /

Thank you, God, for the gift of today. As I honestly review the events of the past 24 hours and pay attention to my feelings, I know your loving presence surrounds me. Bless my journal and our time spent together.

I felt alive in your presence today, God, when...

_____

_____

_____

_____

I struggled to feel your presence today, God, when...

_____

_____

_____

_____

God, I want to share more deeply with you about one moment that stands out from today. Through this experience, I think you might be telling me...

_____

_____

_____

_____

_____

As I think about tomorrow, God, I pray that...

_____

_____

_____

_____

_____

_____

_____ / _____ / _____

Thank you, God, for the gift of today. As I honestly review the events of the past 24 hours and pay attention to my feelings, I know your loving presence surrounds me. Bless my journal and our time spent together.

I felt alive in your presence today, God, when...

_____
_____
_____
_____
_____

I struggled to feel your presence today, God, when...

_____
_____
_____
_____
_____

God, I want to share more deeply with you about one moment that stands out from today. Through this experience, I think you might be telling me...

_____
_____
_____
_____
_____

As I think about tomorrow, God, I pray that...

_____
_____
_____
_____
_____
_____
_____

_____ / _____ / _____

Thank you, God, for the gift of today. As I honestly review the events of the past 24 hours and pay attention to my feelings, I know your loving presence surrounds me. Bless my journal and our time spent together.

I felt alive in your presence today, God, when...

_____

_____

_____

_____

_____

I struggled to feel your presence today, God, when...

_____

_____

_____

_____

God, I want to share more deeply with you about one moment that stands out from today. Through this experience, I think you might be telling me...

_____

_____

_____

_____

_____

As I think about tomorrow, God, I pray that...

_____

_____

_____

_____

_____

_____

_____ / _____ / _____

Thank you, God, for the gift of today. As I honestly review the events of the past 24 hours and pay attention to my feelings, I know your loving presence surrounds me. Bless my journal and our time spent together.

I felt alive in your presence today, God, when...

•

_____

_____

_____

_____

I struggled to feel your presence today, God, when...

_____

_____

_____

_____

God, I want to share more deeply with you about one moment that stands out from today. Through this experience, I think you might be telling me...

_____

_____

_____

_____

_____

As I think about tomorrow, God, I pray that...

_____

_____

_____

_____

_____

_____

_____

_____ / _____ / _____

Thank you, God, for the gift of today. As I honestly review the events of the past 24 hours and pay attention to my feelings, I know your loving presence surrounds me. Bless my journal and our time spent together.

I felt alive in your presence today, God, when...

_____

_____

_____

_____

I struggled to feel your presence today, God, when...

_____

_____

_____

_____

God, I want to share more deeply with you about one moment that stands out from today. Through this experience, I think you might be telling me...

_____

_____

_____

_____

_____

As I think about tomorrow, God, I pray that...

_____

_____

_____

_____

_____

_____

_____ / _____ / _____

Thank you, God, for the gift of today. As I honestly review the events of the past 24 hours and pay attention to my feelings, I know your loving presence surrounds me. Bless my journal and our time spent together.

I felt alive in your presence today, God, when...

_____

_____

_____

_____

_____

I struggled to feel your presence today, God, when...

_____

_____

_____

_____

_____

God, I want to share more deeply with you about one moment that stands out from today. Through this experience, I think you might be telling me...

_____

_____

_____

_____

_____

_____

As I think about tomorrow, God, I pray that...

_____

_____

_____

_____

_____

_____

_____

_____ / _____ / _____

Thank you, God, for the gift of today. As I honestly review the events of the past 24 hours and pay attention to my feelings, I know your loving presence surrounds me. Bless my journal and our time spent together.

I felt alive in your presence today, God, when...

_____

_____

_____

_____

I struggled to feel your presence today, God, when...

_____

_____

_____

_____

God, I want to share more deeply with you about one moment that stands out from today. Through this experience, I think you might be telling me...

_____

_____

_____

_____

_____

As I think about tomorrow, God, I pray that...

_____

_____

_____

_____

_____

_____

_____ / _____ / _____

Thank you, God, for the gift of today. As I honestly review the events of the past 24 hours and pay attention to my feelings, I know your loving presence surrounds me. Bless my journal and our time spent together.

I felt alive in your presence today, God, when...

I struggled to feel your presence today, God, when...

God, I want to share more deeply with you about one moment that stands out from today. Through this experience, I think you might be telling me...

As I think about tomorrow, God, I pray that...

_____ / _____ / _____

Thank you, God, for the gift of today. As I honestly review the events of the past 24 hours and pay attention to my feelings, I know your loving presence surrounds me. Bless my journal and our time spent together.

I felt alive in your presence today, God, when...

_____

_____

_____

_____

I struggled to feel your presence today, God, when...

_____

_____

_____

God, I want to share more deeply with you about one moment that stands out from today. Through this experience, I think you might be telling me...

_____

_____

_____

_____

As I think about tomorrow, God, I pray that...

_____

_____

_____

_____

_____

_____ / _____ / _____

Thank you, God, for the gift of today. As I honestly review the events of the past 24 hours and pay attention to my feelings, I know your loving presence surrounds me. Bless my journal and our time spent together.

I felt alive in your presence today, God, when...

_____
_____
_____
_____

I struggled to feel your presence today, God, when...

_____
_____
_____
_____

God, I want to share more deeply with you about one moment that stands out from today. Through this experience, I think you might be telling me...

_____
_____
_____
_____

As I think about tomorrow, God, I pray that...

_____
_____
_____
_____
_____
_____

_____/_____/_____

Thank you, God, for the gift of today. As I honestly review the events of the past 24 hours and pay attention to my feelings, I know your loving presence surrounds me. Bless my journal and our time spent together.

I felt alive in your presence today, God, when...

_____

_____

_____

_____

I struggled to feel your presence today, God, when...

_____

_____

_____

_____

God, I want to share more deeply with you about one moment that stands out from today. Through this experience, I think you might be telling me...

_____

_____

_____

_____

_____

As I think about tomorrow, God, I pray that...

_____

_____

_____

_____

_____

_____

_____ / _____ / _____

Thank you, God, for the gift of today. As I honestly review the events of the past 24 hours and pay attention to my feelings, I know your loving presence surrounds me. Bless my journal and our time spent together.

I felt alive in your presence today, God, when...

_____

_____

_____

_____

_____

I struggled to feel your presence today, God, when...

_____

_____

_____

_____

God, I want to share more deeply with you about one moment that stands out from today. Through this experience, I think you might be telling me...

_____

_____

_____

_____

_____

As I think about tomorrow, God, I pray that...

_____

_____

_____

_____

_____

_____

_____

_____ / _____ / _____

Thank you, God, for the gift of today. As I honestly review the events of the past 24 hours and pay attention to my feelings, I know your loving presence surrounds me. Bless my journal and our time spent together.

I felt alive in your presence today, God, when...

_____

_____

_____

_____

I struggled to feel your presence today, God, when...

_____

_____

_____

God, I want to share more deeply with you about one moment that stands out from today. Through this experience, I think you might be telling me...

_____

_____

_____

_____

As I think about tomorrow, God, I pray that...

_____

_____

_____

_____

_____

_____

Thank you, God, for the gift of today. As I honestly review the events of the past 24 hours and pay attention to my feelings, I know your loving presence surrounds me. Bless my journal and our time spent together.

I felt alive in your presence today, God, when...

_____

_____

_____

_____

I struggled to feel your presence today, God, when...

_____

_____

_____

_____

God, I want to share more deeply with you about one moment that stands out from today. Through this experience, I think you might be telling me...

_____

_____

_____

_____

As I think about tomorrow, God, I pray that...

_____

_____

_____

_____

_____

_____

_____

_____ / _____ / _____

Thank you, God, for the gift of today. As I honestly review the events of the past 24 hours and pay attention to my feelings, I know your loving presence surrounds me. Bless my journal and our time spent together.

I felt alive in your presence today, God, when...

_____

_____

_____

_____

I struggled to feel your presence today, God, when...

_____

_____

_____

_____

God, I want to share more deeply with you about one moment that stands out from today. Through this experience, I think you might be telling me...

_____

_____

_____

_____

_____

As I think about tomorrow, God, I pray that...

_____

_____

_____

_____

_____

_____

Thank you, God, for the gift of today. As I honestly review the events of the past 24 hours and pay attention to my feelings, I know your loving presence surrounds me. Bless my journal and our time spent together.

I felt alive in your presence today, God, when...

_____

_____

_____

_____

I struggled to feel your presence today, God, when...

_____

_____

_____

God, I want to share more deeply with you about one moment that stands out from today. Through this experience, I think you might be telling me...

_____

_____

_____

_____

As I think about tomorrow, God, I pray that...

_____

_____

_____

_____

_____

_____

Thank you, God, for the gift of today. As I honestly review the events of the past 24 hours and pay attention to my feelings, I know your loving presence surrounds me. Bless my journal and our time spent together.

I felt alive in your presence today, God, when...

_____

_____

_____

_____

I struggled to feel your presence today, God, when...

_____

_____

_____

_____

God, I want to share more deeply with you about one moment that stands out from today. Through this experience, I think you might be telling me...

_____

_____

_____

_____

_____

As I think about tomorrow, God, I pray that...

_____

_____

_____

_____

_____

_____

_____ / _____ / _____

Thank you, God, for the gift of today. As I honestly review the events of the past 24 hours and pay attention to my feelings, I know your loving presence surrounds me. Bless my journal and our time spent together.

I felt alive in your presence today, God, when...

_____

_____

_____

_____

_____

I struggled to feel your presence today, God, when...

_____

_____

_____

_____

God, I want to share more deeply with you about one moment that stands out from today. Through this experience, I think you might be telling me...

_____

_____

_____

_____

_____

As I think about tomorrow, God, I pray that...

_____

_____

_____

_____

_____

_____

_____ / _____ / _____

Thank you, God, for the gift of today. As I honestly review the events of the past 24 hours and pay attention to my feelings, I know your loving presence surrounds me. Bless my journal and our time spent together.

I felt alive in your presence today, God, when...

_____
_____
_____
_____
_____

I struggled to feel your presence today, God, when...

_____
_____
_____
_____

God, I want to share more deeply with you about one moment that stands out from today. Through this experience, I think you might be telling me...

_____
_____
_____
_____
_____

As I think about tomorrow, God, I pray that...

_____
_____
_____
_____
_____
_____

I wish not merely
to be called Christian,
but also to

be

Christian.

- St. Ignatius

_____/_____/_____

Thank you, God, for the gift of today. As I honestly review the events of the past 24 hours and pay attention to my feelings, I know your loving presence surrounds me. Bless my journal and our time spent together.

I felt alive in your presence today, God, when...

I struggled to feel your presence today, God, when...

God, I want to share more deeply with you about one moment that stands out from today. Through this experience, I think you might be telling me...

As I think about tomorrow, God, I pray that...

Thank you, God, for the gift of today. As I honestly review the events of the past 24 hours and pay attention to my feelings, I know your loving presence surrounds me. Bless my journal and our time spent together.

I felt alive in your presence today, God, when...

I struggled to feel your presence today, God, when...

God, I want to share more deeply with you about one moment that stands out from today. Through this experience, I think you might be telling me...

As I think about tomorrow, God, I pray that...

_____/_____/_____

Thank you, God, for the gift of today. As I honestly review the events of the past 24 hours and pay attention to my feelings, I know your loving presence surrounds me. Bless my journal and our time spent together.

I felt alive in your presence today, God, when...

_____

_____

_____

_____

I struggled to feel your presence today, God, when...

_____

_____

_____

_____

God, I want to share more deeply with you about one moment that stands out from today. Through this experience, I think you might be telling me...

_____

_____

_____

_____

As I think about tomorrow, God, I pray that...

_____

_____

_____

_____

_____

_____

_____ / _____ / _____

Thank you, God, for the gift of today. As I honestly review the events of the past 24 hours and pay attention to my feelings, I know your loving presence surrounds me. Bless my journal and our time spent together.

I felt alive in your presence today, God, when...

_____

_____

_____

_____

I struggled to feel your presence today, God, when...

_____

_____

_____

_____

God, I want to share more deeply with you about one moment that stands out from today. Through this experience, I think you might be telling me...

_____

_____

_____

_____

_____

As I think about tomorrow, God, I pray that...

_____

_____

_____

_____

_____

_____

_____

_____ / _____ / _____

Thank you, God, for the gift of today. As I honestly review the events of the past 24 hours and pay attention to my feelings, I know your loving presence surrounds me. Bless my journal and our time spent together.

I felt alive in your presence today, God, when...

_____

_____

_____

_____

I struggled to feel your presence today, God, when...

_____

_____

_____

God, I want to share more deeply with you about one moment that stands out from today. Through this experience, I think you might be telling me...

_____

_____

_____

_____

As I think about tomorrow, God, I pray that...

_____

_____

_____

_____

_____

_____ / _____ / _____

Thank you, God, for the gift of today. As I honestly review the events of the past 24 hours and pay attention to my feelings, I know your loving presence surrounds me. Bless my journal and our time spent together.

I felt alive in your presence today, God, when...

_____

_____

_____

_____

I struggled to feel your presence today, God, when...

_____

_____

_____

_____

God, I want to share more deeply with you about one moment that stands out from today. Through this experience, I think you might be telling me...

_____

_____

_____

_____

As I think about tomorrow, God, I pray that...

_____

_____

_____

_____

_____

_____

_____ / _____ /

Thank you, God, for the gift of today. As I honestly review the events of the past 24 hours and pay attention to my feelings, I know your loving presence surrounds me. Bless my journal and our time spent together.

I felt alive in your presence today, God, when...

_____

_____

_____

_____

I struggled to feel your presence today, God, when...

_____

_____

_____

_____

God, I want to share more deeply with you about one moment that stands out from today. Through this experience, I think you might be telling me...

_____

_____

_____

_____

_____

As I think about tomorrow, God, I pray that...

_____

_____

_____

_____

_____

_____

_____

Thank you, God, for the gift of today. As I honestly review the events of the past 24 hours and pay attention to my feelings, I know your loving presence surrounds me. Bless my journal and our time spent together.

I felt alive in your presence today, God, when...

_____

_____

_____

_____

I struggled to feel your presence today, God, when...

_____

_____

_____

_____

God, I want to share more deeply with you about one moment that stands out from today. Through this experience, I think you might be telling me...

_____

_____

_____

_____

As I think about tomorrow, God, I pray that...

_____

_____

_____

_____

_____

_____

_____ / _____ / _____

Thank you, God, for the gift of today. As I honestly review the events of the past 24 hours and pay attention to my feelings, I know your loving presence surrounds me. Bless my journal and our time spent together.

I felt alive in your presence today, God, when...

_____

_____

_____

_____

I struggled to feel your presence today, God, when...

_____

_____

_____

_____

God, I want to share more deeply with you about one moment that stands out from today. Through this experience, I think you might be telling me...

_____

_____

_____

_____

_____

As I think about tomorrow, God, I pray that...

_____

_____

_____

_____

_____

_____

Thank you, God, for the gift of today. As I honestly review the events of the past 24 hours and pay attention to my feelings, I know your loving presence surrounds me. Bless my journal and our time spent together.

I felt alive in your presence today, God, when...

_____

_____

_____

_____

_____

I struggled to feel your presence today, God, when...

_____

_____

_____

_____

_____

God, I want to share more deeply with you about one moment that stands out from today. Through this experience, I think you might be telling me...

_____

_____

_____

_____

_____

As I think about tomorrow, God, I pray that...

_____

_____

_____

_____

_____

_____

_____

_____/_____/_____

Thank you, God, for the gift of today. As I honestly review the events of the past 24 hours and pay attention to my feelings, I know your loving presence surrounds me. Bless my journal and our time spent together.

I felt alive in your presence today, God, when...

_____

_____

_____

_____

I struggled to feel your presence today, God, when...

_____

_____

_____

_____

God, I want to share more deeply with you about one moment that stands out from today. Through this experience, I think you might be telling me...

_____

_____

_____

_____

_____

As I think about tomorrow, God, I pray that...

_____

_____

_____

_____

_____

_____

_____ / _____ / _____

Thank you, God, for the gift of today. As I honestly review the events of the past 24 hours and pay attention to my feelings, I know your loving presence surrounds me. Bless my journal and our time spent together.

I felt alive in your presence today, God, when...

_____
_____
_____
_____
_____

I struggled to feel your presence today, God, when...

_____
_____
_____
_____
_____

God, I want to share more deeply with you about one moment that stands out from today. Through this experience, I think you might be telling me...

_____
_____
_____
_____
_____

As I think about tomorrow, God, I pray that...

_____
_____
_____
_____
_____
_____
_____

Thank you, God, for the gift of today. As I honestly review the events of the past 24 hours and pay attention to my feelings, I know your loving presence surrounds me. Bless my journal and our time spent together.

I felt alive in your presence today, God, when...

_____

_____

_____

_____

_____

I struggled to feel your presence today, God, when...

_____

_____

_____

_____

_____

God, I want to share more deeply with you about one moment that stands out from today. Through this experience, I think you might be telling me...

_____

_____

_____

_____

_____

As I think about tomorrow, God, I pray that...

_____

_____

_____

_____

_____

_____

_____ / _____ / _____

Thank you, God, for the gift of today. As I honestly review the events of the past 24 hours and pay attention to my feelings, I know your loving presence surrounds me. Bless my journal and our time spent together.

I felt alive in your presence today, God, when...

_____

_____

_____

_____

_____

I struggled to feel your presence today, God, when...

_____

_____

_____

_____

_____

God, I want to share more deeply with you about one moment that stands out from today. Through this experience, I think you might be telling me...

_____

_____

_____

_____

_____

As I think about tomorrow, God, I pray that...

_____

_____

_____

_____

_____

_____

_____

_____ / _____ / _____

Thank you, God, for the gift of today. As I honestly review the events of the past 24 hours and pay attention to my feelings, I know your loving presence surrounds me. Bless my journal and our time spent together.

I felt alive in your presence today, God, when...

_____

_____

_____

_____

I struggled to feel your presence today, God, when...

_____

_____

_____

_____

God, I want to share more deeply with you about one moment that stands out from today. Through this experience, I think you might be telling me...

_____

_____

_____

_____

_____

As I think about tomorrow, God, I pray that...

_____

_____

_____

_____

_____

_____

Thank you, God, for the gift of today. As I honestly review the events of the past 24 hours and pay attention to my feelings, I know your loving presence surrounds me. Bless my journal and our time spent together.

I felt alive in your presence today, God, when...

I struggled to feel your presence today, God, when...

God, I want to share more deeply with you about one moment that stands out from today. Through this experience, I think you might be telling me...

As I think about tomorrow, God, I pray that...

Thank you, God, for the gift of today. As I honestly review the events of the past 24 hours and pay attention to my feelings, I know your loving presence surrounds me. Bless my journal and our time spent together.

I felt alive in your presence today, God, when...

_____

_____

_____

_____

I struggled to feel your presence today, God, when...

_____

_____

_____

God, I want to share more deeply with you about one moment that stands out from today. Through this experience, I think you might be telling me...

_____

_____

_____

_____

As I think about tomorrow, God, I pray that...

_____

_____

_____

_____

_____

_____

Thank you, God, for the gift of today. As I honestly review the events of the past 24 hours and pay attention to my feelings, I know your loving presence surrounds me. Bless my journal and our time spent together.

I felt alive in your presence today, God, when...

I struggled to feel your presence today, God, when...

God, I want to share more deeply with you about one moment that stands out from today. Through this experience, I think you might be telling me...

As I think about tomorrow, God, I pray that...

_____ / _____ / _____

Thank you, God, for the gift of today. As I honestly review the events of the past 24 hours and pay attention to my feelings, I know your loving presence surrounds me. Bless my journal and our time spent together.

I felt alive in your presence today, God, when...

_____

_____

_____

_____

_____

I struggled to feel your presence today, God, when...

_____

_____

_____

_____

_____

God, I want to share more deeply with you about one moment that stands out from today. Through this experience, I think you might be telling me...

_____

_____

_____

_____

_____

_____

As I think about tomorrow, God, I pray that...

_____

_____

_____

_____

_____

_____

_____

_____ / _____ / _____

Thank you, God, for the gift of today. As I honestly review the events of the past 24 hours and pay attention to my feelings, I know your loving presence surrounds me. Bless my journal and our time spent together.

I felt alive in your presence today, God, when...

_____

_____

_____

_____

I struggled to feel your presence today, God, when...

_____

_____

_____

_____

God, I want to share more deeply with you about one moment that stands out from today. Through this experience, I think you might be telling me...

_____

_____

_____

_____

_____

As I think about tomorrow, God, I pray that...

_____

_____

_____

_____

_____

_____

Thank you, God, for the gift of today. As I honestly review the events of the past 24 hours and pay attention to my feelings, I know your loving presence surrounds me. Bless my journal and our time spent together.

I felt alive in your presence today, God, when...

I struggled to feel your presence today, God, when...

God, I want to share more deeply with you about one moment that stands out from today. Through this experience, I think you might be telling me...

As I think about tomorrow, God, I pray that...

Thank you, God, for the gift of today. As I honestly review the events of the past 24 hours and pay attention to my feelings, I know your loving presence surrounds me. Bless my journal and our time spent together.

I felt alive in your presence today, God, when...

_____ •

_____

_____

_____

I struggled to feel your presence today, God, when...

_____

_____

_____

_____

God, I want to share more deeply with you about one moment that stands out from today. Through this experience, I think you might be telling me...

_____

_____

_____

_____

_____

As I think about tomorrow, God, I pray that...

_____

_____

_____

_____

_____

_____

_____

_____ / _____ / _____

Thank you, God, for the gift of today. As I honestly review the events of the past 24 hours and pay attention to my feelings, I know your loving presence surrounds me. Bless my journal and our time spent together.

I felt alive in your presence today, God, when...

_____

_____

_____

_____

I struggled to feel your presence today, God, when...

_____

_____

_____

God, I want to share more deeply with you about one moment that stands out from today. Through this experience, I think you might be telling me...

_____

_____

_____

_____

As I think about tomorrow, God, I pray that...

_____

_____

_____

_____

_____

_____

Thank you, God, for the gift of today. As I honestly review the events of the past 24 hours and pay attention to my feelings, I know your loving presence surrounds me. Bless my journal and our time spent together.

I felt alive in your presence today, God, when...

I struggled to feel your presence today, God, when...

God, I want to share more deeply with you about one moment that stands out from today. Through this experience, I think you might be telling me...

As I think about tomorrow, God, I pray that...

_____ / _____ / _____

Thank you, God, for the gift of today. As I honestly review the events of the past 24 hours and pay attention to my feelings, I know your loving presence surrounds me. Bless my journal and our time spent together.

I felt alive in your presence today, God, when...

_____
_____
_____
_____
_____

I struggled to feel your presence today, God, when...

_____
_____
_____
_____

God, I want to share more deeply with you about one moment that stands out from today. Through this experience, I think you might be telling me...

_____
_____
_____
_____
_____

As I think about tomorrow, God, I pray that...

_____
_____
_____
_____
_____
_____
_____

_____ / _____ / _____

Thank you, God, for the gift of today. As I honestly review the events of the past 24 hours and pay attention to my feelings, I know your loving presence surrounds me. Bless my journal and our time spent together.

I felt alive in your presence today, God, when...

_____

_____

_____

_____

I struggled to feel your presence today, God, when...

_____

_____

_____

_____

God, I want to share more deeply with you about one moment that stands out from today. Through this experience, I think you might be telling me...

_____

_____

_____

_____

_____

As I think about tomorrow, God, I pray that...

_____

_____

_____

_____

_____

_____

_____/_____/_____

Thank you, God, for the gift of today. As I honestly review the events of the past 24 hours and pay attention to my feelings, I know your loving presence surrounds me. Bless my journal and our time spent together.

I felt alive in your presence today, God, when...

_____

_____

_____

_____

I struggled to feel your presence today, God, when...

_____

_____

_____

_____

God, I want to share more deeply with you about one moment that stands out from today. Through this experience, I think you might be telling me...

_____

_____

_____

_____

_____

As I think about tomorrow, God, I pray that...

_____

_____

_____

_____

_____

_____

_____ / _____ / _____

Thank you, God, for the gift of today. As I honestly review the events of the past 24 hours and pay attention to my feelings, I know your loving presence surrounds me. Bless my journal and our time spent together.

I felt alive in your presence today, God, when...

_____

_____

_____

_____

I struggled to feel your presence today, God, when...

_____

_____

_____

_____

God, I want to share more deeply with you about one moment that stands out from today. Through this experience, I think you might be telling me...

_____

_____

_____

_____

As I think about tomorrow, God, I pray that...

_____

_____

_____

_____

_____

_____

_____ / _____ / _____

Thank you, God, for the gift of today. As I honestly review the events of the past 24 hours and pay attention to my feelings, I know your loving presence surrounds me. Bless my journal and our time spent together.

I felt alive in your presence today, God, when...

_____

_____

_____

_____

I struggled to feel your presence today, God, when...

_____

_____

_____

_____

God, I want to share more deeply with you about one moment that stands out from today. Through this experience, I think you might be telling me...

_____

_____

_____

_____

_____

As I think about tomorrow, God, I pray that...

_____

_____

_____

_____

_____

_____

_____/_____/_____

Thank you, God, for the gift of today. As I honestly review the events of the past 24 hours and pay attention to my feelings, I know your loving presence surrounds me. Bless my journal and our time spent together.

I felt alive in your presence today, God, when...

_____

_____

_____

_____

_____

I struggled to feel your presence today, God, when...

_____

_____

_____

_____

God, I want to share more deeply with you about one moment that stands out from today. Through this experience, I think you might be telling me...

_____

_____

_____

_____

_____

As I think about tomorrow, God, I pray that...

_____

_____

_____

_____

_____

_____

_____

_____ / _____ / _____

Thank you, God, for the gift of today. As I honestly review the events of the past 24 hours and pay attention to my feelings, I know your loving presence surrounds me. Bless my journal and our time spent together.

I felt alive in your presence today, God, when...

_____

_____

_____

_____

I struggled to feel your presence today, God, when...

_____

_____

_____

_____

God, I want to share more deeply with you about one moment that stands out from today. Through this experience, I think you might be telling me...

_____

_____

_____

_____

_____

As I think about tomorrow, God, I pray that...

_____

_____

_____

_____

_____

_____

_____ / _____ / _____

Thank you, God, for the gift of today. As I honestly review the events of the past 24 hours and pay attention to my feelings, I know your loving presence surrounds me. Bless my journal and our time spent together.

I felt alive in your presence today, God, when...

_____

_____

_____

_____

I struggled to feel your presence today, God, when...

_____

_____

_____

_____

God, I want to share more deeply with you about one moment that stands out from today. Through this experience, I think you might be telling me...

_____

_____

_____

_____

_____

As I think about tomorrow, God, I pray that...

_____

_____

_____

_____

_____

_____

_____

Lord, teach me
to be generous.
Teach me to serve you as you deserve;
to give and not to count the cost,
to fight and not to heed the wounds,
to toil and not to seek for rest,
to labor and not to ask for reward,
save that of knowing
that I do your will.

- St. Ignatius

Thank you, God, for the gift of today. As I honestly review the events of the past 24 hours and pay attention to my feelings, I know your loving presence surrounds me. Bless my journal and our time spent together.

I felt alive in your presence today, God, when...

I struggled to feel your presence today, God, when...

God, I want to share more deeply with you about one moment that stands out from today. Through this experience, I think you might be telling me...

As I think about tomorrow, God, I pray that...

_____ / _____ /

Thank you, God, for the gift of today. As I honestly review the events of the past 24 hours and pay attention to my feelings, I know your loving presence surrounds me. Bless my journal and our time spent together.

I felt alive in your presence today, God, when...

_____

_____

_____

_____

I struggled to feel your presence today, God, when...

_____

_____

_____

_____

God, I want to share more deeply with you about one moment that stands out from today. Through this experience, I think you might be telling me...

_____

_____

_____

_____

_____

As I think about tomorrow, God, I pray that...

_____

_____

_____

_____

_____

_____

Thank you, God, for the gift of today. As I honestly review the events of the past 24 hours and pay attention to my feelings, I know your loving presence surrounds me. Bless my journal and our time spent together.

I felt alive in your presence today, God, when...

I struggled to feel your presence today, God, when...

God, I want to share more deeply with you about one moment that stands out from today. Through this experience, I think you might be telling me...

As I think about tomorrow, God, I pray that...

Thank you, God, for the gift of today. As I honestly review the events of the past 24 hours and pay attention to my feelings, I know your loving presence surrounds me. Bless my journal and our time spent together.

I felt alive in your presence today, God, when...

_____

_____

_____

_____

I struggled to feel your presence today, God, when...

_____

_____

_____

_____

God, I want to share more deeply with you about one moment that stands out from today. Through this experience, I think you might be telling me...

_____

_____

_____

_____

_____

As I think about tomorrow, God, I pray that...

_____

_____

_____

_____

_____

_____

_____ / _____ / _____

Thank you, God, for the gift of today. As I honestly review the events of the past 24 hours and pay attention to my feelings, I know your loving presence surrounds me. Bless my journal and our time spent together.

I felt alive in your presence today, God, when...

_____

_____

_____

_____

I struggled to feel your presence today, God, when...

_____

_____

_____

_____

God, I want to share more deeply with you about one moment that stands out from today. Through this experience, I think you might be telling me...

_____

_____

_____

_____

_____

As I think about tomorrow, God, I pray that...

_____

_____

_____

_____

_____

_____

_____ / _____ / _____

Thank you, God, for the gift of today. As I honestly review the events of the past 24 hours and pay attention to my feelings, I know your loving presence surrounds me. Bless my journal and our time spent together.

I felt alive in your presence today, God, when...

_____

_____

_____

_____

I struggled to feel your presence today, God, when...

_____

_____

_____

_____

God, I want to share more deeply with you about one moment that stands out from today. Through this experience, I think you might be telling me...

_____

_____

_____

_____

_____

As I think about tomorrow, God, I pray that...

_____

_____

_____

_____

_____

_____

Thank you, God, for the gift of today. As I honestly review the events of the past 24 hours and pay attention to my feelings, I know your loving presence surrounds me. Bless my journal and our time spent together.

I felt alive in your presence today, God, when...

I struggled to feel your presence today, God, when...

God, I want to share more deeply with you about one moment that stands out from today. Through this experience, I think you might be telling me...

As I think about tomorrow, God, I pray that...

_____ / _____ /

Thank you, God, for the gift of today. As I honestly review the events of the past 24 hours and pay attention to my feelings, I know your loving presence surrounds me. Bless my journal and our time spent together.

I felt alive in your presence today, God, when...

_____

_____

_____

_____

I struggled to feel your presence today, God, when...

_____

_____

_____

_____

God, I want to share more deeply with you about one moment that stands out from today. Through this experience, I think you might be telling me...

_____

_____

_____

_____

_____

As I think about tomorrow, God, I pray that...

_____

_____

_____

_____

_____

_____

Thank you, God, for the gift of today. As I honestly review the events of the past 24 hours and pay attention to my feelings, I know your loving presence surrounds me. Bless my journal and our time spent together.

I felt alive in your presence today, God, when...

_____

_____

_____

_____

I struggled to feel your presence today, God, when...

_____

_____

_____

_____

God, I want to share more deeply with you about one moment that stands out from today. Through this experience, I think you might be telling me...

_____

_____

_____

_____

_____

As I think about tomorrow, God, I pray that...

_____

_____

_____

_____

_____

_____

_____ / _____ /

Thank you, God, for the gift of today. As I honestly review the events of the past 24 hours and pay attention to my feelings, I know your loving presence surrounds me. Bless my journal and our time spent together.

I felt alive in your presence today, God, when...

_____

_____

_____

_____

I struggled to feel your presence today, God, when...

_____

_____

_____

_____

God, I want to share more deeply with you about one moment that stands out from today. Through this experience, I think you might be telling me...

_____

_____

_____

_____

_____

As I think about tomorrow, God, I pray that...

_____

_____

_____

_____

_____

_____

_____

Thank you, God, for the gift of today. As I honestly review the events of the past 24 hours and pay attention to my feelings, I know your loving presence surrounds me. Bless my journal and our time spent together.

I felt alive in your presence today, God, when...

_____

_____

_____

_____

I struggled to feel your presence today, God, when...

_____

_____

_____

_____

God, I want to share more deeply with you about one moment that stands out from today. Through this experience, I think you might be telling me...

_____

_____

_____

_____

_____

As I think about tomorrow, God, I pray that...

_____

_____

_____

_____

_____

_____

_____ / _____ / _____

Thank you, God, for the gift of today. As I honestly review the events of the past 24 hours and pay attention to my feelings, I know your loving presence surrounds me. Bless my journal and our time spent together.

I felt alive in your presence today, God, when...

_____

_____

_____

_____

_____

I struggled to feel your presence today, God, when...

_____

_____

_____

_____

God, I want to share more deeply with you about one moment that stands out from today. Through this experience, I think you might be telling me...

_____

_____

_____

_____

_____

As I think about tomorrow, God, I pray that...

_____

_____

_____

_____

_____

_____

_____

_____ / _____ / _____

Thank you, God, for the gift of today. As I honestly review the events of the past 24 hours and pay attention to my feelings, I know your loving presence surrounds me. Bless my journal and our time spent together.

I felt alive in your presence today, God, when...

_____

_____

_____

_____

I struggled to feel your presence today, God, when...

_____

_____

_____

_____

God, I want to share more deeply with you about one moment that stands out from today. Through this experience, I think you might be telling me...

_____

_____

_____

_____

As I think about tomorrow, God, I pray that...

_____

_____

_____

_____

_____

_____

_____ / _____ / _____

Thank you, God, for the gift of today. As I honestly review the events of the past 24 hours and pay attention to my feelings, I know your loving presence surrounds me. Bless my journal and our time spent together.

I felt alive in your presence today, God, when...

_____

_____

_____

_____

I struggled to feel your presence today, God, when...

_____

_____

_____

_____

God, I want to share more deeply with you about one moment that stands out from today. Through this experience, I think you might be telling me...

_____

_____

_____

_____

_____

As I think about tomorrow, God, I pray that...

_____

_____

_____

_____

_____

_____

_____ / _____ / _____

Thank you, God, for the gift of today. As I honestly review the events of the past 24 hours and pay attention to my feelings, I know your loving presence surrounds me. Bless my journal and our time spent together.

I felt alive in your presence today, God, when...

_____

_____

_____

_____

I struggled to feel your presence today, God, when...

_____

_____

_____

_____

God, I want to share more deeply with you about one moment that stands out from today. Through this experience, I think you might be telling me...

_____

_____

_____

_____

As I think about tomorrow, God, I pray that...

_____

_____

_____

_____

_____

_____

_____/_____/_____

Thank you, God, for the gift of today. As I honestly review the events of the past 24 hours and pay attention to my feelings, I know your loving presence surrounds me. Bless my journal and our time spent together.

I felt alive in your presence today, God, when...

_____

_____

_____

_____

I struggled to feel your presence today, God, when...

_____

_____

_____

God, I want to share more deeply with you about one moment that stands out from today. Through this experience, I think you might be telling me...

_____

_____

_____

_____

As I think about tomorrow, God, I pray that...

_____

_____

_____

_____

_____

_____ / _____ / _____

Thank you, God, for the gift of today. As I honestly review the events of the past 24 hours and pay attention to my feelings, I know your loving presence surrounds me. Bless my journal and our time spent together.

I felt alive in your presence today, God, when...

_____

_____

_____

_____

I struggled to feel your presence today, God, when...

_____

_____

_____

_____

God, I want to share more deeply with you about one moment that stands out from today. Through this experience, I think you might be telling me...

_____

_____

_____

_____

As I think about tomorrow, God, I pray that...

_____

_____

_____

_____

_____

_____

Thank you, God, for the gift of today. As I honestly review the events of the past 24 hours and pay attention to my feelings, I know your loving presence surrounds me. Bless my journal and our time spent together.

I felt alive in your presence today, God, when...

_____

_____

_____

_____

I struggled to feel your presence today, God, when...

_____

_____

_____

_____

God, I want to share more deeply with you about one moment that stands out from today. Through this experience, I think you might be telling me...

_____

_____

_____

_____

_____

As I think about tomorrow, God, I pray that...

_____

_____

_____

_____

_____

_____

_____

_____ / _____ / _____

Thank you, God, for the gift of today. As I honestly review the events of the past 24 hours and pay attention to my feelings, I know your loving presence surrounds me. Bless my journal and our time spent together.

I felt alive in your presence today, God, when...

_____

_____

_____

_____

I struggled to feel your presence today, God, when...

_____

_____

_____

_____

God, I want to share more deeply with you about one moment that stands out from today. Through this experience, I think you might be telling me...

_____

_____

_____

_____

_____

As I think about tomorrow, God, I pray that...

_____

_____

_____

_____

_____

_____

_____ / _____ / _____

Thank you, God, for the gift of today. As I honestly review the events of the past 24 hours and pay attention to my feelings, I know your loving presence surrounds me. Bless my journal and our time spent together.

I felt alive in your presence today, God, when...

_____
_____
_____
_____

I struggled to feel your presence today, God, when...

_____
_____
_____
_____

God, I want to share more deeply with you about one moment that stands out from today. Through this experience, I think you might be telling me...

_____
_____
_____
_____

As I think about tomorrow, God, I pray that...

_____
_____
_____
_____
_____
_____

Thank you, God, for the gift of today. As I honestly review the events of the past 24 hours and pay attention to my feelings, I know your loving presence surrounds me. Bless my journal and our time spent together.

I felt alive in your presence today, God, when...

_____

_____

_____

_____

I struggled to feel your presence today, God, when...

_____

_____

_____

_____

God, I want to share more deeply with you about one moment that stands out from today. Through this experience, I think you might be telling me...

_____

_____

_____

_____

_____

As I think about tomorrow, God, I pray that...

_____

_____

_____

_____

_____

_____

_____ / _____ / _____

Thank you, God, for the gift of today. As I honestly review the events of the past 24 hours and pay attention to my feelings, I know your loving presence surrounds me. Bless my journal and our time spent together.

I felt alive in your presence today, God, when...

_____

_____

_____

_____

I struggled to feel your presence today, God, when...

_____

_____

_____

_____

God, I want to share more deeply with you about one moment that stands out from today. Through this experience, I think you might be telling me...

_____

_____

_____

_____

_____

As I think about tomorrow, God, I pray that...

_____

_____

_____

_____

_____

_____

_____ / _____ / _____

Thank you, God, for the gift of today. As I honestly review the events of the past 24 hours and pay attention to my feelings, I know your loving presence surrounds me. Bless my journal and our time spent together.

I felt alive in your presence today, God, when...

....
....
....
....
....

I struggled to feel your presence today, God, when...

....
....
....
....

God, I want to share more deeply with you about one moment that stands out from today. Through this experience, I think you might be telling me...

....
....
....
....
....

As I think about tomorrow, God, I pray that...

....
....
....
....
....
....
....

_____ / _____ / _____

Thank you, God, for the gift of today. As I honestly review the events of the past 24 hours and pay attention to my feelings, I know your loving presence surrounds me. Bless my journal and our time spent together.

I felt alive in your presence today, God, when...

_____

_____

_____

_____

I struggled to feel your presence today, God, when...

_____

_____

_____

_____

God, I want to share more deeply with you about one moment that stands out from today. Through this experience, I think you might be telling me...

_____

_____

_____

_____

_____

As I think about tomorrow, God, I pray that...

_____

_____

_____

_____

_____

_____

_____ / _____ / _____

Thank you, God, for the gift of today. As I honestly review the events of the past 24 hours and pay attention to my feelings, I know your loving presence surrounds me. Bless my journal and our time spent together.

I felt alive in your presence today, God, when...

_____

_____

_____

_____

_____

I struggled to feel your presence today, God, when...

_____

_____

_____

_____

_____

God, I want to share more deeply with you about one moment that stands out from today. Through this experience, I think you might be telling me...

_____

_____

_____

_____

_____

As I think about tomorrow, God, I pray that...

_____

_____

_____

_____

_____

_____

_____

_____ / _____ / _____

Thank you, God, for the gift of today. As I honestly review the events of the past 24 hours and pay attention to my feelings, I know your loving presence surrounds me. Bless my journal and our time spent together.

I felt alive in your presence today, God, when...

_____

_____

_____

_____

I struggled to feel your presence today, God, when...

_____

_____

_____

_____

God, I want to share more deeply with you about one moment that stands out from today. Through this experience, I think you might be telling me...

_____

_____

_____

_____

_____

As I think about tomorrow, God, I pray that...

_____

_____

_____

_____

_____

_____

_____ / _____ / _____

Thank you, God, for the gift of today. As I honestly review the events of the past 24 hours and pay attention to my feelings, I know your loving presence surrounds me. Bless my journal and our time spent together.

I felt alive in your presence today, God, when...

_____

_____ •

_____

_____

_____

I struggled to feel your presence today, God, when...

_____

_____

_____

_____

God, I want to share more deeply with you about one moment that stands out from today. Through this experience, I think you might be telling me...

_____

_____

_____

_____

_____

As I think about tomorrow, God, I pray that...

_____

_____

_____

_____

_____

_____

_____

_____ / _____ /

Thank you, God, for the gift of today. As I honestly review the events of the past 24 hours and pay attention to my feelings, I know your loving presence surrounds me. Bless my journal and our time spent together.

I felt alive in your presence today, God, when...

_____

_____

_____

_____

I struggled to feel your presence today, God, when...

_____

_____

_____

_____

God, I want to share more deeply with you about one moment that stands out from today. Through this experience, I think you might be telling me...

_____

_____

_____

_____

As I think about tomorrow, God, I pray that...

_____

_____

_____

_____

_____

_____

_____ / _____ / _____

Thank you, God, for the gift of today. As I honestly review the events of the past 24 hours and pay attention to my feelings, I know your loving presence surrounds me. Bless my journal and our time spent together.

I felt alive in your presence today, God, when...

_____

_____

_____

_____

I struggled to feel your presence today, God, when...

_____

_____

_____

_____

God, I want to share more deeply with you about one moment that stands out from today. Through this experience, I think you might be telling me...

_____

_____

_____

_____

_____

As I think about tomorrow, God, I pray that...

_____

_____

_____

_____

_____

_____

_____

_____ / _____ / _____

Thank you, God, for the gift of today. As I honestly review the events of the past 24 hours and pay attention to my feelings, I know your loving presence surrounds me. Bless my journal and our time spent together.

I felt alive in your presence today, God, when...

_____
_____
_____
_____
_____

I struggled to feel your presence today, God, when...

_____
_____
_____
_____

God, I want to share more deeply with you about one moment that stands out from today. Through this experience, I think you might be telling me...

_____
_____
_____
_____
_____

As I think about tomorrow, God, I pray that...

_____
_____
_____
_____
_____
_____
_____

Thank you, God, for the gift of today. As I honestly review the events of the past 24 hours and pay attention to my feelings, I know your loving presence surrounds me. Bless my journal and our time spent together.

I felt alive in your presence today, God, when...

_____

_____

_____

_____

I struggled to feel your presence today, God, when...

_____

_____

_____

_____

God, I want to share more deeply with you about one moment that stands out from today. Through this experience, I think you might be telling me...

_____

_____

_____

_____

_____

As I think about tomorrow, God, I pray that...

_____

_____

_____

_____

_____

_____

_____ / _____ / _____

Thank you, God, for the gift of today. As I honestly review the events of the past 24 hours and pay attention to my feelings, I know your loving presence surrounds me. Bless my journal and our time spent together.

I felt alive in your presence today, God, when...

_____

_____

_____

_____

I struggled to feel your presence today, God, when...

_____

_____

_____

_____

God, I want to share more deeply with you about one moment that stands out from today. Through this experience, I think you might be telling me...

_____

_____

_____

_____

_____

As I think about tomorrow, God, I pray that...

_____

_____

_____

_____

_____

_____

_____ / _____ / _____

Thank you, God, for the gift of today. As I honestly review the events of the past 24 hours and pay attention to my feelings, I know your loving presence surrounds me. Bless my journal and our time spent together.

I felt alive in your presence today, God, when...

_____

_____

_____

_____

I struggled to feel your presence today, God, when...

_____

_____

_____

_____

God, I want to share more deeply with you about one moment that stands out from today. Through this experience, I think you might be telling me...

_____

_____

_____

_____

_____

As I think about tomorrow, God, I pray that...

_____

_____

_____

_____

_____

_____

laugh
and
grow
strong

- St. Ignatius

_____ / _____ / _____

Thank you, God, for the gift of today. As I honestly review the events of the past 24 hours and pay attention to my feelings, I know your loving presence surrounds me. Bless my journal and our time spent together.

I felt alive in your presence today, God, when...

_____

_____

_____

_____

I struggled to feel your presence today, God, when...

_____

_____

_____

_____

God, I want to share more deeply with you about one moment that stands out from today. Through this experience, I think you might be telling me...

_____

_____

_____

_____

As I think about tomorrow, God, I pray that...

_____

_____

_____

_____

_____

_____

_____/_____/_____

Thank you, God, for the gift of today. As I honestly review the events of the past 24 hours and pay attention to my feelings, I know your loving presence surrounds me. Bless my journal and our time spent together.

I felt alive in your presence today, God, when...

_____

_____

_____

_____

I struggled to feel your presence today, God, when...

_____

_____

_____

_____

God, I want to share more deeply with you about one moment that stands out from today. Through this experience, I think you might be telling me...

_____

_____

_____

_____

_____

As I think about tomorrow, God, I pray that...

_____

_____

_____

_____

_____

_____

_____ / _____ / _____

Thank you, God, for the gift of today. As I honestly review the events of the past 24 hours and pay attention to my feelings, I know your loving presence surrounds me. Bless my journal and our time spent together.

I felt alive in your presence today, God, when...

_____

_____

_____

_____

I struggled to feel your presence today, God, when...

_____

_____

_____

_____

God, I want to share more deeply with you about one moment that stands out from today. Through this experience, I think you might be telling me...

_____

_____

_____

_____

_____

As I think about tomorrow, God, I pray that...

_____

_____

_____

_____

_____

_____

Thank you, God, for the gift of today. As I honestly review the events of the past 24 hours and pay attention to my feelings, I know your loving presence surrounds me. Bless my journal and our time spent together.

I felt alive in your presence today, God, when...

_____

_____

_____

_____

_____

I struggled to feel your presence today, God, when...

_____

_____

_____

_____

God, I want to share more deeply with you about one moment that stands out from today. Through this experience, I think you might be telling me...

_____

_____

_____

_____

_____

As I think about tomorrow, God, I pray that...

_____

_____

_____

_____

_____

_____

_____

_____ / _____ / _____

Thank you, God, for the gift of today. As I honestly review the events of the past 24 hours and pay attention to my feelings, I know your loving presence surrounds me. Bless my journal and our time spent together.

I felt alive in your presence today, God, when...

_____

_____

_____

_____

I struggled to feel your presence today, God, when...

_____

_____

_____

_____

God, I want to share more deeply with you about one moment that stands out from today. Through this experience, I think you might be telling me...

_____

_____

_____

_____

_____

As I think about tomorrow, God, I pray that...

_____

_____

_____

_____

_____

_____

_____/_____/_____

Thank you, God, for the gift of today. As I honestly review the events of the past 24 hours and pay attention to my feelings, I know your loving presence surrounds me. Bless my journal and our time spent together.

I felt alive in your presence today, God, when...

_____
_____
_____
_____

I struggled to feel your presence today, God, when...

_____
_____
_____

God, I want to share more deeply with you about one moment that stands out from today. Through this experience, I think you might be telling me...

_____
_____
_____
_____

As I think about tomorrow, God, I pray that...

_____
_____
_____
_____
_____

Thank you, God, for the gift of today. As I honestly review the events of the past 24 hours and pay attention to my feelings, I know your loving presence surrounds me. Bless my journal and our time spent together.

I felt alive in your presence today, God, when...

I struggled to feel your presence today, God, when...

God, I want to share more deeply with you about one moment that stands out from today. Through this experience, I think you might be telling me...

As I think about tomorrow, God, I pray that...

_____ / _____ / _____

Thank you, God, for the gift of today. As I honestly review the events of the past 24 hours and pay attention to my feelings, I know your loving presence surrounds me. Bless my journal and our time spent together.

I felt alive in your presence today, God, when...

_____

_____

_____

_____

_____

I struggled to feel your presence today, God, when...

_____

_____

_____

_____

God, I want to share more deeply with you about one moment that stands out from today. Through this experience, I think you might be telling me...

_____

_____

_____

_____

_____

As I think about tomorrow, God, I pray that...

_____

_____

_____

_____

_____

_____

_____

_____ / _____ / _____

Thank you, God, for the gift of today. As I honestly review the events of the past 24 hours and pay attention to my feelings, I know your loving presence surrounds me. Bless my journal and our time spent together.

I felt alive in your presence today, God, when...

_____

_____

_____

_____

I struggled to feel your presence today, God, when...

_____

_____

_____

_____

God, I want to share more deeply with you about one moment that stands out from today. Through this experience, I think you might be telling me...

_____

_____

_____

_____

_____

As I think about tomorrow, God, I pray that...

_____

_____

_____

_____

_____

_____

_____

_____ / _____ /

Thank you, God, for the gift of today. As I honestly review the events of the past 24 hours and pay attention to my feelings, I know your loving presence surrounds me. Bless my journal and our time spent together.

I felt alive in your presence today, God, when...

_____

_____

_____

_____

I struggled to feel your presence today, God, when...

_____

_____

_____

_____

God, I want to share more deeply with you about one moment that stands out from today. Through this experience, I think you might be telling me...

_____

_____

_____

_____

_____

As I think about tomorrow, God, I pray that...

_____

_____

_____

_____

_____

_____

_____ / _____ / _____

Thank you, God, for the gift of today. As I honestly review the events of the past 24 hours and pay attention to my feelings, I know your loving presence surrounds me. Bless my journal and our time spent together.

I felt alive in your presence today, God, when...

_____

_____

_____

_____

I struggled to feel your presence today, God, when...

_____

_____

_____

_____

God, I want to share more deeply with you about one moment that stands out from today. Through this experience, I think you might be telling me...

_____

_____

_____

_____

_____

As I think about tomorrow, God, I pray that...

_____

_____

_____

_____

_____

_____

_____

_____/_____/_____

Thank you, God, for the gift of today. As I honestly review the events of the past 24 hours and pay attention to my feelings, I know your loving presence surrounds me. Bless my journal and our time spent together.

I felt alive in your presence today, God, when...

_____

_____

_____

_____

I struggled to feel your presence today, God, when...

_____

_____

_____

_____

God, I want to share more deeply with you about one moment that stands out from today. Through this experience, I think you might be telling me...

_____

_____

_____

_____

As I think about tomorrow, God, I pray that...

_____

_____

_____

_____

_____

_____

_____ / _____ / _____

Thank you, God, for the gift of today. As I honestly review the events of the past 24 hours and pay attention to my feelings, I know your loving presence surrounds me. Bless my journal and our time spent together.

I felt alive in your presence today, God, when...

_____

_____

_____

_____

_____

I struggled to feel your presence today, God, when...

_____

_____

_____

_____

_____

God, I want to share more deeply with you about one moment that stands out from today. Through this experience, I think you might be telling me...

_____

_____

_____

_____

_____

As I think about tomorrow, God, I pray that...

_____

_____

_____

_____

_____

_____

_____

Thank you, God, for the gift of today. As I honestly review the events of the past 24 hours and pay attention to my feelings, I know your loving presence surrounds me. Bless my journal and our time spent together.

I felt alive in your presence today, God, when...

_____

_____

_____

_____

_____

I struggled to feel your presence today, God, when...

_____

_____

_____

_____

_____

God, I want to share more deeply with you about one moment that stands out from today. Through this experience, I think you might be telling me...

_____

_____

_____

_____

_____

As I think about tomorrow, God, I pray that...

_____

_____

_____

_____

_____

_____

_____ / _____ / _____

Thank you, God, for the gift of today. As I honestly review the events of the past 24 hours and pay attention to my feelings, I know your loving presence surrounds me. Bless my journal and our time spent together.

I felt alive in your presence today, God, when...

I struggled to feel your presence today, God, when...

God, I want to share more deeply with you about one moment that stands out from today. Through this experience, I think you might be telling me...

As I think about tomorrow, God, I pray that...

_____/_____/_____

Thank you, God, for the gift of today. As I honestly review the events of the past 24 hours and pay attention to my feelings, I know your loving presence surrounds me. Bless my journal and our time spent together.

I felt alive in your presence today, God, when...

_____

_____

_____

_____

I struggled to feel your presence today, God, when...

_____

_____

_____

_____

God, I want to share more deeply with you about one moment that stands out from today. Through this experience, I think you might be telling me...

_____

_____

_____

_____

_____

As I think about tomorrow, God, I pray that...

_____

_____

_____

_____

_____

_____

Thank you, God, for the gift of today. As I honestly review the events of the past 24 hours and pay attention to my feelings, I know your loving presence surrounds me. Bless my journal and our time spent together.

I felt alive in your presence today, God, when...

_____

_____

_____

_____

I struggled to feel your presence today, God, when...

_____

_____

_____

_____

God, I want to share more deeply with you about one moment that stands out from today. Through this experience, I think you might be telling me...

_____

_____

_____

_____

_____

As I think about tomorrow, God, I pray that...

_____

_____

_____

_____

_____

_____

_____

_____/_____/_____

Thank you, God, for the gift of today. As I honestly review the events of the past 24 hours and pay attention to my feelings, I know your loving presence surrounds me. Bless my journal and our time spent together.

I felt alive in your presence today, God, when...

I struggled to feel your presence today, God, when...

God, I want to share more deeply with you about one moment that stands out from today. Through this experience, I think you might be telling me...

As I think about tomorrow, God, I pray that...

Thank you, God, for the gift of today. As I honestly review the events of the past 24 hours and pay attention to my feelings, I know your loving presence surrounds me. Bless my journal and our time spent together.

I felt alive in your presence today, God, when...

I struggled to feel your presence today, God, when...

God, I want to share more deeply with you about one moment that stands out from today. Through this experience, I think you might be telling me...

As I think about tomorrow, God, I pray that...

_____ / _____ / _____

Thank you, God, for the gift of today. As I honestly review the events of the past 24 hours and pay attention to my feelings, I know your loving presence surrounds me. Bless my journal and our time spent together.

I felt alive in your presence today, God, when...

_____

_____

_____

_____

I struggled to feel your presence today, God, when...

_____

_____

_____

_____

God, I want to share more deeply with you about one moment that stands out from today. Through this experience, I think you might be telling me...

_____

_____

_____

_____

_____

As I think about tomorrow, God, I pray that...

_____

_____

_____

_____

_____

_____

_____ / _____ / _____

Thank you, God, for the gift of today. As I honestly review the events of the past 24 hours and pay attention to my feelings, I know your loving presence surrounds me. Bless my journal and our time spent together.

I felt alive in your presence today, God, when...

_____

_____

_____

_____

I struggled to feel your presence today, God, when...

_____

_____

_____

_____

God, I want to share more deeply with you about one moment that stands out from today. Through this experience, I think you might be telling me...

_____

_____

_____

_____

_____

As I think about tomorrow, God, I pray that...

_____

_____

_____

_____

_____

_____

_____ / _____ / _____

Thank you, God, for the gift of today. As I honestly review the events of the past 24 hours and pay attention to my feelings, I know your loving presence surrounds me. Bless my journal and our time spent together.

I felt alive in your presence today, God, when...

_____

_____

_____

_____

I struggled to feel your presence today, God, when...

_____

_____

_____

_____

God, I want to share more deeply with you about one moment that stands out from today. Through this experience, I think you might be telling me...

_____

_____

_____

_____

_____

As I think about tomorrow, God, I pray that...

_____

_____

_____

_____

_____

_____

_____ / _____ / _____

Thank you, God, for the gift of today. As I honestly review the events of the past 24 hours and pay attention to my feelings, I know your loving presence surrounds me. Bless my journal and our time spent together.

I felt alive in your presence today, God, when...

_____

_____

_____

_____

I struggled to feel your presence today, God, when...

_____

_____

_____

_____

God, I want to share more deeply with you about one moment that stands out from today. Through this experience, I think you might be telling me...

_____

_____

_____

_____

_____

As I think about tomorrow, God, I pray that...

_____

_____

_____

_____

_____

_____

_____ / _____ / _____

Thank you, God, for the gift of today. As I honestly review the events of the past 24 hours and pay attention to my feelings, I know your loving presence surrounds me. Bless my journal and our time spent together.

I felt alive in your presence today, God, when...

_____

_____

_____

_____

I struggled to feel your presence today, God, when...

_____

_____

_____

_____

God, I want to share more deeply with you about one moment that stands out from today. Through this experience, I think you might be telling me...

_____

_____

_____

_____

As I think about tomorrow, God, I pray that...

_____

_____

_____

_____

_____

_____

_____ / _____ / _____

Thank you, God, for the gift of today. As I honestly review the events of the past 24 hours and pay attention to my feelings, I know your loving presence surrounds me. Bless my journal and our time spent together.

I felt alive in your presence today, God, when...

_____
_____
_____
_____

I struggled to feel your presence today, God, when...

_____
_____
_____
_____

God, I want to share more deeply with you about one moment that stands out from today. Through this experience, I think you might be telling me...

_____
_____
_____
_____
_____

As I think about tomorrow, God, I pray that...

_____
_____
_____
_____
_____
_____
_____

_____ / _____ / _____

Thank you, God, for the gift of today. As I honestly review the events of the past 24 hours and pay attention to my feelings, I know your loving presence surrounds me. Bless my journal and our time spent together.

I felt alive in your presence today, God, when...

_____

_____

_____

_____

I struggled to feel your presence today, God, when...

_____

_____

_____

God, I want to share more deeply with you about one moment that stands out from today. Through this experience, I think you might be telling me...

_____

_____

_____

_____

As I think about tomorrow, God, I pray that...

_____

_____

_____

_____

_____

_____

Thank you, God, for the gift of today. As I honestly review the events of the past 24 hours and pay attention to my feelings, I know your loving presence surrounds me. Bless my journal and our time spent together.

I felt alive in your presence today, God, when...

_____

_____

_____

_____

_____

I struggled to feel your presence today, God, when...

_____

_____

_____

_____

_____

God, I want to share more deeply with you about one moment that stands out from today. Through this experience, I think you might be telling me...

_____

_____

_____

_____

_____

As I think about tomorrow, God, I pray that...

_____

_____

_____

_____

_____

_____

_____

_____ / _____ /

Thank you, God, for the gift of today. As I honestly review the events of the past 24 hours and pay attention to my feelings, I know your loving presence surrounds me. Bless my journal and our time spent together.

I felt alive in your presence today, God, when...

_____

_____

_____

_____

_____

I struggled to feel your presence today, God, when...

_____

_____

_____

_____

God, I want to share more deeply with you about one moment that stands out from today. Through this experience, I think you might be telling me...

_____

_____

_____

_____

_____

As I think about tomorrow, God, I pray that...

_____

_____

_____

_____

_____

_____

_____

_____/_____/_____

Thank you, God, for the gift of today. As I honestly review the events of the past 24 hours and pay attention to my feelings, I know your loving presence surrounds me. Bless my journal and our time spent together.

I felt alive in your presence today, God, when...

_____

_____

_____

_____

I struggled to feel your presence today, God, when...

_____

_____

_____

God, I want to share more deeply with you about one moment that stands out from today. Through this experience, I think you might be telling me...

_____

_____

_____

_____

As I think about tomorrow, God, I pray that...

_____

_____

_____

_____

_____

_____

Thank you, God, for the gift of today. As I honestly review the events of the past 24 hours and pay attention to my feelings, I know your loving presence surrounds me. Bless my journal and our time spent together.

I felt alive in your presence today, God, when...

_____

_____

_____

_____

_____

I struggled to feel your presence today, God, when...

_____

_____

_____

_____

God, I want to share more deeply with you about one moment that stands out from today. Through this experience, I think you might be telling me...

_____

_____

_____

_____

_____

As I think about tomorrow, God, I pray that...

_____

_____

_____

_____

_____

_____

_____ / _____ / _____

Thank you, God, for the gift of today. As I honestly review the events of the past 24 hours and pay attention to my feelings, I know your loving presence surrounds me. Bless my journal and our time spent together.

I felt alive in your presence today, God, when...

_____
_____
_____
_____

I struggled to feel your presence today, God, when...

_____
_____
_____
_____

God, I want to share more deeply with you about one moment that stands out from today. Through this experience, I think you might be telling me...

_____
_____
_____
_____
_____

As I think about tomorrow, God, I pray that...

_____
_____
_____
_____
_____
_____

May the
perfect grace
and
eternal love
of Christ our Lord
be our never-failing
protection and help.

- St. Ignatius

_____ / _____ / _____

Thank you, God, for the gift of today. As I honestly review the events of the past 24 hours and pay attention to my feelings, I know your loving presence surrounds me. Bless my journal and our time spent together.

I felt alive in your presence today, God, when...

_____

_____

_____

_____

_____

I struggled to feel your presence today, God, when...

_____

_____

_____

_____

God, I want to share more deeply with you about one moment that stands out from today. Through this experience, I think you might be telling me...

_____

_____

_____

_____

As I think about tomorrow, God, I pray that...

_____

_____

_____

_____

_____

_____

_____/_____/_____

Thank you, God, for the gift of today. As I honestly review the events of the past 24 hours and pay attention to my feelings, I know your loving presence surrounds me. Bless my journal and our time spent together.

I felt alive in your presence today, God, when...

_____

_____

_____

_____

I struggled to feel your presence today, God, when...

_____

_____

_____

_____

God, I want to share more deeply with you about one moment that stands out from today. Through this experience, I think you might be telling me...

_____

_____

_____

_____

_____

As I think about tomorrow, God, I pray that...

_____

_____

_____

_____

_____

_____

_____ / _____ /

Thank you, God, for the gift of today. As I honestly review the events of the past 24 hours and pay attention to my feelings, I know your loving presence surrounds me. Bless my journal and our time spent together.

I felt alive in your presence today, God, when...

_____
_____
_____
_____

I struggled to feel your presence today, God, when...

_____
_____
_____
_____

God, I want to share more deeply with you about one moment that stands out from today. Through this experience, I think you might be telling me...

_____
_____
_____
_____

As I think about tomorrow, God, I pray that...

_____
_____
_____
_____
_____

_____ / _____ / _____

Thank you, God, for the gift of today. As I honestly review the events of the past 24 hours and pay attention to my feelings, I know your loving presence surrounds me. Bless my journal and our time spent together.

I felt alive in your presence today, God, when...

_____

_____

_____

_____

I struggled to feel your presence today, God, when...

_____

_____

_____

_____

God, I want to share more deeply with you about one moment that stands out from today. Through this experience, I think you might be telling me...

_____

_____

_____

_____

_____

As I think about tomorrow, God, I pray that...

_____

_____

_____

_____

_____

_____

_____/_____/_____

Thank you, God, for the gift of today. As I honestly review the events of the past 24 hours and pay attention to my feelings, I know your loving presence surrounds me. Bless my journal and our time spent together.

I felt alive in your presence today, God, when...

_____

_____

_____

_____

_____

I struggled to feel your presence today, God, when...

_____

_____

_____

_____

God, I want to share more deeply with you about one moment that stands out from today. Through this experience, I think you might be telling me...

_____

_____

_____

_____

_____

As I think about tomorrow, God, I pray that...

_____

_____

_____

_____

_____

_____

_____

_____ / _____ / _____

Thank you, God, for the gift of today. As I honestly review the events of the past 24 hours and pay attention to my feelings, I know your loving presence surrounds me. Bless my journal and our time spent together.

I felt alive in your presence today, God, when...

_____

_____

_____

_____

I struggled to feel your presence today, God, when...

_____

_____

_____

_____

God, I want to share more deeply with you about one moment that stands out from today. Through this experience, I think you might be telling me...

_____

_____

_____

_____

As I think about tomorrow, God, I pray that...

_____

_____

_____

_____

_____

_____

Thank you, God, for the gift of today. As I honestly review the events of the past 24 hours and pay attention to my feelings, I know your loving presence surrounds me. Bless my journal and our time spent together.

I felt alive in your presence today, God, when...

_____

_____

_____

_____

_____

I struggled to feel your presence today, God, when...

_____

_____

_____

_____

God, I want to share more deeply with you about one moment that stands out from today. Through this experience, I think you might be telling me...

_____

_____

_____

_____

_____

As I think about tomorrow, God, I pray that...

_____

_____

_____

_____

_____

_____

_____

_____ / _____ / _____

Thank you, God, for the gift of today. As I honestly review the events of the past 24 hours and pay attention to my feelings, I know your loving presence surrounds me. Bless my journal and our time spent together.

I felt alive in your presence today, God, when...

_____

_____

_____

_____

I struggled to feel your presence today, God, when...

_____

_____

_____

_____

God, I want to share more deeply with you about one moment that stands out from today. Through this experience, I think you might be telling me...

_____

_____

_____

_____

_____

As I think about tomorrow, God, I pray that...

_____

_____

_____

_____

_____

_____

_____ / _____ /

Thank you, God, for the gift of today. As I honestly review the events of the past 24 hours and pay attention to my feelings, I know your loving presence surrounds me. Bless my journal and our time spent together.

I felt alive in your presence today, God, when...

I struggled to feel your presence today, God, when...

God, I want to share more deeply with you about one moment that stands out from today. Through this experience, I think you might be telling me...

As I think about tomorrow, God, I pray that...

_____ / _____ / _____

Thank you, God, for the gift of today. As I honestly review the events of the past 24 hours and pay attention to my feelings, I know your loving presence surrounds me. Bless my journal and our time spent together.

I felt alive in your presence today, God, when...

_____

_____

_____

_____

I struggled to feel your presence today, God, when...

_____

_____

_____

_____

God, I want to share more deeply with you about one moment that stands out from today. Through this experience, I think you might be telling me...

_____

_____

_____

_____

_____

As I think about tomorrow, God, I pray that...

_____

_____

_____

_____

_____

_____

Thank you, God, for the gift of today. As I honestly review the events of the past 24 hours and pay attention to my feelings, I know your loving presence surrounds me. Bless my journal and our time spent together.

I felt alive in your presence today, God, when...

_____

_____

_____

_____

I struggled to feel your presence today, God, when...

_____

_____

_____

_____

God, I want to share more deeply with you about one moment that stands out from today. Through this experience, I think you might be telling me...

_____

_____

_____

_____

As I think about tomorrow, God, I pray that...

_____

_____

_____

_____

_____

_____

_____ / _____ /

Thank you, God, for the gift of today. As I honestly review the events of the past 24 hours and pay attention to my feelings, I know your loving presence surrounds me. Bless my journal and our time spent together.

I felt alive in your presence today, God, when...

_____

_____

_____

_____

I struggled to feel your presence today, God, when...

_____

_____

_____

_____

God, I want to share more deeply with you about one moment that stands out from today. Through this experience, I think you might be telling me...

_____

_____

_____

_____

As I think about tomorrow, God, I pray that...

_____

_____

_____

_____

_____

_____

_____ / _____ / _____

Thank you, God, for the gift of today. As I honestly review the events of the past 24 hours and pay attention to my feelings, I know your loving presence surrounds me. Bless my journal and our time spent together.

I felt alive in your presence today, God, when...

_____

_____

_____

_____

I struggled to feel your presence today, God, when...

_____

_____

_____

_____

God, I want to share more deeply with you about one moment that stands out from today. Through this experience, I think you might be telling me...

_____

_____

_____

_____

_____

As I think about tomorrow, God, I pray that...

_____

_____

_____

_____

_____

_____

_____ / _____ / _____

Thank you, God, for the gift of today. As I honestly review the events of the past 24 hours and pay attention to my feelings, I know your loving presence surrounds me. Bless my journal and our time spent together.

I felt alive in your presence today, God, when...

_____

_____

_____

_____

I struggled to feel your presence today, God, when...

_____

_____

_____

_____

God, I want to share more deeply with you about one moment that stands out from today. Through this experience, I think you might be telling me...

_____

_____

_____

_____

_____

As I think about tomorrow, God, I pray that...

_____

_____

_____

_____

_____

_____

_____ / _____ / _____

Thank you, God, for the gift of today. As I honestly review the events of the past 24 hours and pay attention to my feelings, I know your loving presence surrounds me. Bless my journal and our time spent together.

I felt alive in your presence today, God, when...

I struggled to feel your presence today, God, when...

God, I want to share more deeply with you about one moment that stands out from today. Through this experience, I think you might be telling me...

As I think about tomorrow, God, I pray that...

_____ / _____ / _____

Thank you, God, for the gift of today. As I honestly review the events of the past 24 hours and pay attention to my feelings, I know your loving presence surrounds me. Bless my journal and our time spent together.

I felt alive in your presence today, God, when...

_____

_____

_____

_____

I struggled to feel your presence today, God, when...

_____

_____

_____

_____

God, I want to share more deeply with you about one moment that stands out from today. Through this experience, I think you might be telling me...

_____

_____

_____

_____

_____

As I think about tomorrow, God, I pray that...

_____

_____

_____

_____

_____

_____

_____

_____ / _____ /

Thank you, God, for the gift of today. As I honestly review the events of the past 24 hours and pay attention to my feelings, I know your loving presence surrounds me. Bless my journal and our time spent together.

I felt alive in your presence today, God, when...

_____

_____

_____

_____

I struggled to feel your presence today, God, when...

_____

_____

_____

_____

God, I want to share more deeply with you about one moment that stands out from today. Through this experience, I think you might be telling me...

_____

_____

_____

_____

As I think about tomorrow, God, I pray that...

_____

_____

_____

_____

_____

_____

_____ / _____ / _____

Thank you, God, for the gift of today. As I honestly review the events of the past 24 hours and pay attention to my feelings, I know your loving presence surrounds me. Bless my journal and our time spent together.

I felt alive in your presence today, God, when...

_____

_____

_____

_____

I struggled to feel your presence today, God, when...

_____

_____

_____

God, I want to share more deeply with you about one moment that stands out from today. Through this experience, I think you might be telling me...

_____

_____

_____

_____

As I think about tomorrow, God, I pray that...

_____

_____

_____

_____

_____

_____

_____ / _____ / _____

Thank you, God, for the gift of today. As I honestly review the events of the past 24 hours and pay attention to my feelings, I know your loving presence surrounds me. Bless my journal and our time spent together.

I felt alive in your presence today, God, when...

_____

_____

_____

_____

I struggled to feel your presence today, God, when...

_____

_____

_____

God, I want to share more deeply with you about one moment that stands out from today. Through this experience, I think you might be telling me...

_____

_____

_____

_____

As I think about tomorrow, God, I pray that...

_____

_____

_____

_____

_____

_____

_____ / _____ / _____

Thank you, God, for the gift of today. As I honestly review the events of the past 24 hours and pay attention to my feelings, I know your loving presence surrounds me. Bless my journal and our time spent together.

I felt alive in your presence today, God, when...

_____

_____

_____

_____

I struggled to feel your presence today, God, when...

_____

_____

_____

_____

God, I want to share more deeply with you about one moment that stands out from today. Through this experience, I think you might be telling me...

_____

_____

_____

_____

As I think about tomorrow, God, I pray that...

_____

_____

_____

_____

_____

_____

_____ / _____ / _____

Thank you, God, for the gift of today. As I honestly review the events of the past 24 hours and pay attention to my feelings, I know your loving presence surrounds me. Bless my journal and our time spent together.

I felt alive in your presence today, God, when...

I struggled to feel your presence today, God, when...

God, I want to share more deeply with you about one moment that stands out from today. Through this experience, I think you might be telling me...

As I think about tomorrow, God, I pray that...

_____ / _____ / _____

Thank you, God, for the gift of today. As I honestly review the events of the past 24 hours and pay attention to my feelings, I know your loving presence surrounds me. Bless my journal and our time spent together.

I felt alive in your presence today, God, when...

_____

_____

_____

_____

I struggled to feel your presence today, God, when...

_____

_____

_____

_____

God, I want to share more deeply with you about one moment that stands out from today. Through this experience, I think you might be telling me...

_____

_____

_____

_____

_____

As I think about tomorrow, God, I pray that...

_____

_____

_____

_____

_____

_____

Thank you, God, for the gift of today. As I honestly review the events of the past 24 hours and pay attention to my feelings, I know your loving presence surrounds me. Bless my journal and our time spent together.

I felt alive in your presence today, God, when...

_____

_____

_____

_____

I struggled to feel your presence today, God, when...

_____

_____

_____

_____

God, I want to share more deeply with you about one moment that stands out from today. Through this experience, I think you might be telling me...

_____

_____

_____

_____

As I think about tomorrow, God, I pray that...

_____

_____

_____

_____

_____

_____

_____ / _____ / _____

Thank you, God, for the gift of today. As I honestly review the events of the past 24 hours and pay attention to my feelings, I know your loving presence surrounds me. Bless my journal and our time spent together.

I felt alive in your presence today, God, when...

_____
_____
_____
_____
_____

I struggled to feel your presence today, God, when...

_____
_____
_____
_____

God, I want to share more deeply with you about one moment that stands out from today. Through this experience, I think you might be telling me...

_____
_____
_____
_____
_____

As I think about tomorrow, God, I pray that...

_____
_____
_____
_____
_____
_____

_____ / _____ /

Thank you, God, for the gift of today. As I honestly review the events of the past 24 hours and pay attention to my feelings, I know your loving presence surrounds me. Bless my journal and our time spent together.

I felt alive in your presence today, God, when...

_____
_____
_____
_____

I struggled to feel your presence today, God, when...

_____
_____
_____
_____

God, I want to share more deeply with you about one moment that stands out from today. Through this experience, I think you might be telling me...

_____
_____
_____
_____
_____

As I think about tomorrow, God, I pray that...

_____
_____
_____
_____
_____
_____

_____/_____/_____

Thank you, God, for the gift of today. As I honestly review the events of the past 24 hours and pay attention to my feelings, I know your loving presence surrounds me. Bless my journal and our time spent together.

I felt alive in your presence today, God, when...

_____
_____
_____
_____
_____

I struggled to feel your presence today, God, when...

_____
_____
_____
_____
_____

God, I want to share more deeply with you about one moment that stands out from today. Through this experience, I think you might be telling me...

_____
_____
_____
_____
_____

As I think about tomorrow, God, I pray that...

_____
_____
_____
_____
_____
_____
_____

_____/_____/_____

Thank you, God, for the gift of today. As I honestly review the events of the past 24 hours and pay attention to my feelings, I know your loving presence surrounds me. Bless my journal and our time spent together.

I felt alive in your presence today, God, when...

_____

_____

_____

_____

_____

I struggled to feel your presence today, God, when...

_____

_____

_____

_____

God, I want to share more deeply with you about one moment that stands out from today. Through this experience, I think you might be telling me...

_____

_____

_____

_____

_____

As I think about tomorrow, God, I pray that...

_____

_____

_____

_____

_____

_____

_____ / _____ / _____

Thank you, God, for the gift of today. As I honestly review the events of the past 24 hours and pay attention to my feelings, I know your loving presence surrounds me. Bless my journal and our time spent together.

I felt alive in your presence today, God, when...

_____

_____

_____

_____

I struggled to feel your presence today, God, when...

_____

_____

_____

_____

God, I want to share more deeply with you about one moment that stands out from today. Through this experience, I think you might be telling me...

_____

_____

_____

_____

_____

As I think about tomorrow, God, I pray that...

_____

_____

_____

_____

_____

_____

_____

_____ / _____ /

Thank you, God, for the gift of today. As I honestly review the events of the past 24 hours and pay attention to my feelings, I know your loving presence surrounds me. Bless my journal and our time spent together.

I felt alive in your presence today, God, when...

_____

_____

_____

_____

I struggled to feel your presence today, God, when...

_____

_____

_____

_____

God, I want to share more deeply with you about one moment that stands out from today. Through this experience, I think you might be telling me...

_____

_____

_____

_____

As I think about tomorrow, God, I pray that...

_____

_____

_____

_____

_____

_____

_____ / _____ / _____

Thank you, God, for the gift of today. As I honestly review the events of the past 24 hours and pay attention to my feelings, I know your loving presence surrounds me. Bless my journal and our time spent together.

I felt alive in your presence today, God, when...

_____

_____

_____

_____

_____

I struggled to feel your presence today, God, when...

_____

_____

_____

_____

God, I want to share more deeply with you about one moment that stands out from today. Through this experience, I think you might be telling me...

_____

_____

_____

_____

_____

As I think about tomorrow, God, I pray that...

_____

_____

_____

_____

_____

_____

TRY TO KEEP YOUR SOUL
ALWAYS IN PEACE AND QUIET,
ALWAYS READY FOR
WHATEVER OUR LORD
MAY WISH TO WORK IN YOU.
IT IS CERTAINLY
A HIGHER VIRTUE OF THE SOUL,
AND A GREATER GRACE,
TO BE ABLE TO ENJOY THE LORD
IN DIFFERENT TIMES
AND DIFFERENT PLACES
THAN IN ONLY ONE.

- ST. IGNATIUS

_____ / _____ / _____

Thank you, God, for the gift of today. As I honestly review the events of the past 24 hours and pay attention to my feelings, I know your loving presence surrounds me. Bless my journal and our time spent together.

I felt alive in your presence today, God, when...

_____

_____

_____

_____

I struggled to feel your presence today, God, when...

_____

_____

_____

God, I want to share more deeply with you about one moment that stands out from today. Through this experience, I think you might be telling me...

_____

_____

_____

_____

As I think about tomorrow, God, I pray that...

_____

_____

_____

_____

_____

_____

_____ / _____ /

Thank you, God, for the gift of today. As I honestly review the events of the past 24 hours and pay attention to my feelings, I know your loving presence surrounds me. Bless my journal and our time spent together.

I felt alive in your presence today, God, when...

_____

_____

_____

_____

I struggled to feel your presence today, God, when...

_____

_____

_____

_____

God, I want to share more deeply with you about one moment that stands out from today. Through this experience, I think you might be telling me...

_____

_____

_____

_____

_____

As I think about tomorrow, God, I pray that...

_____

_____

_____

_____

_____

_____

_____ / _____ / _____

Thank you, God, for the gift of today. As I honestly review the events of the past 24 hours and pay attention to my feelings, I know your loving presence surrounds me. Bless my journal and our time spent together.

I felt alive in your presence today, God, when...

I struggled to feel your presence today, God, when...

God, I want to share more deeply with you about one moment that stands out from today. Through this experience, I think you might be telling me...

As I think about tomorrow, God, I pray that...

_____ / _____ / _____

Thank you, God, for the gift of today. As I honestly review the events of the past 24 hours and pay attention to my feelings, I know your loving presence surrounds me. Bless my journal and our time spent together.

I felt alive in your presence today, God, when...

_____

_____

_____

_____

I struggled to feel your presence today, God, when...

_____

_____

_____

_____

God, I want to share more deeply with you about one moment that stands out from today. Through this experience, I think you might be telling me...

_____

_____

_____

_____

_____

As I think about tomorrow, God, I pray that...

_____

_____

_____

_____

_____

_____

_____

_____ / _____ / _____

Thank you, God, for the gift of today. As I honestly review the events of the past 24 hours and pay attention to my feelings, I know your loving presence surrounds me. Bless my journal and our time spent together.

I felt alive in your presence today, God, when...

_____

_____

_____

_____

_____

I struggled to feel your presence today, God, when...

_____

_____

_____

_____

_____

God, I want to share more deeply with you about one moment that stands out from today. Through this experience, I think you might be telling me...

_____

_____

_____

_____

_____

_____

As I think about tomorrow, God, I pray that...

_____

_____

_____

_____

_____

_____

_____

_____ / _____ / _____

Thank you, God, for the gift of today. As I honestly review the events of the past 24 hours and pay attention to my feelings, I know your loving presence surrounds me. Bless my journal and our time spent together.

I felt alive in your presence today, God, when...

_____

_____

_____

_____

_____

I struggled to feel your presence today, God, when...

_____

_____

_____

_____

God, I want to share more deeply with you about one moment that stands out from today. Through this experience, I think you might be telling me...

_____

_____

_____

_____

_____

As I think about tomorrow, God, I pray that...

_____

_____

_____

_____

_____

_____

_____ / _____ / _____

Thank you, God, for the gift of today. As I honestly review the events of the past 24 hours and pay attention to my feelings, I know your loving presence surrounds me. Bless my journal and our time spent together.

I felt alive in your presence today, God, when...

_____

_____

_____

_____

I struggled to feel your presence today, God, when...

_____

_____

_____

_____

God, I want to share more deeply with you about one moment that stands out from today. Through this experience, I think you might be telling me...

_____

_____

_____

_____

_____

As I think about tomorrow, God, I pray that...

_____

_____

_____

_____

_____

_____

_____/_____/_____

Thank you, God, for the gift of today. As I honestly review the events of the past 24 hours and pay attention to my feelings, I know your loving presence surrounds me. Bless my journal and our time spent together.

I felt alive in your presence today, God, when...

_____

_____

_____

_____

I struggled to feel your presence today, God, when...

_____

_____

_____

God, I want to share more deeply with you about one moment that stands out from today. Through this experience, I think you might be telling me...

_____

_____

_____

_____

As I think about tomorrow, God, I pray that...

_____

_____

_____

_____

_____

_____

_____/_____/_____

Thank you, God, for the gift of today. As I honestly review the events of the past 24 hours and pay attention to my feelings, I know your loving presence surrounds me. Bless my journal and our time spent together.

I felt alive in your presence today, God, when...

_____

_____

_____

_____

_____

I struggled to feel your presence today, God, when...

_____

_____

_____

_____

God, I want to share more deeply with you about one moment that stands out from today. Through this experience, I think you might be telling me...

_____

_____

_____

_____

_____

As I think about tomorrow, God, I pray that...

_____

_____

_____

_____

_____

_____

_____

_____ / _____ / _____

Thank you, God, for the gift of today. As I honestly review the events of the past 24 hours and pay attention to my feelings, I know your loving presence surrounds me. Bless my journal and our time spent together.

I felt alive in your presence today, God, when...

_____

_____

_____

_____

I struggled to feel your presence today, God, when...

_____

_____

_____

_____

God, I want to share more deeply with you about one moment that stands out from today. Through this experience, I think you might be telling me...

_____

_____

_____

_____

_____

As I think about tomorrow, God, I pray that...

_____

_____

_____

_____

_____

_____

_____ / _____ / _____

Thank you, God, for the gift of today. As I honestly review the events of the past 24 hours and pay attention to my feelings, I know your loving presence surrounds me. Bless my journal and our time spent together.

I felt alive in your presence today, God, when...

_____

_____

_____

_____

I struggled to feel your presence today, God, when...

_____

_____

_____

_____

God, I want to share more deeply with you about one moment that stands out from today. Through this experience, I think you might be telling me...

_____

_____

_____

_____

_____

As I think about tomorrow, God, I pray that...

_____

_____

_____

_____

_____

_____

_____ / _____ / _____

Thank you, God, for the gift of today. As I honestly review the events of the past 24 hours and pay attention to my feelings, I know your loving presence surrounds me. Bless my journal and our time spent together.

I felt alive in your presence today, God, when...

_____

_____

_____

_____

I struggled to feel your presence today, God, when...

_____

_____

_____

_____

God, I want to share more deeply with you about one moment that stands out from today. Through this experience, I think you might be telling me...

_____

_____

_____

_____

As I think about tomorrow, God, I pray that...

_____

_____

_____

_____

_____

_____

_____/_____/_____

Thank you, God, for the gift of today. As I honestly review the events of the past 24 hours and pay attention to my feelings, I know your loving presence surrounds me. Bless my journal and our time spent together.

I felt alive in your presence today, God, when...

_____

_____

_____

_____

I struggled to feel your presence today, God, when...

_____

_____

_____

_____

God, I want to share more deeply with you about one moment that stands out from today. Through this experience, I think you might be telling me...

_____

_____

_____

_____

_____

As I think about tomorrow, God, I pray that...

_____

_____

_____

_____

_____

_____

_____ / _____ / _____

Thank you, God, for the gift of today. As I honestly review the events of the past 24 hours and pay attention to my feelings, I know your loving presence surrounds me. Bless my journal and our time spent together.

I felt alive in your presence today, God, when...

_____

_____

_____

_____

_____

I struggled to feel your presence today, God, when...

_____

_____

_____

_____

God, I want to share more deeply with you about one moment that stands out from today. Through this experience, I think you might be telling me...

_____

_____

_____

_____

_____

As I think about tomorrow, God, I pray that...

_____

_____

_____

_____

_____

_____

Thank you, God, for the gift of today. As I honestly review the events of the past 24 hours and pay attention to my feelings, I know your loving presence surrounds me. Bless my journal and our time spent together.

I felt alive in your presence today, God, when...

I struggled to feel your presence today, God, when...

God, I want to share more deeply with you about one moment that stands out from today. Through this experience, I think you might be telling me...

As I think about tomorrow, God, I pray that...

_____ / _____ /

Thank you, God, for the gift of today. As I honestly review the events of the past 24 hours and pay attention to my feelings, I know your loving presence surrounds me. Bless my journal and our time spent together.

I felt alive in your presence today, God, when...

_____

_____

_____

_____

I struggled to feel your presence today, God, when...

_____

_____

_____

_____

God, I want to share more deeply with you about one moment that stands out from today. Through this experience, I think you might be telling me...

_____

_____

_____

_____

As I think about tomorrow, God, I pray that...

_____

_____

_____

_____

_____

_____

_____ / _____ / _____

Thank you, God, for the gift of today. As I honestly review the events of the past 24 hours and pay attention to my feelings, I know your loving presence surrounds me. Bless my journal and our time spent together.

I felt alive in your presence today, God, when...

_____

_____

_____

_____

I struggled to feel your presence today, God, when...

_____

_____

_____

_____

God, I want to share more deeply with you about one moment that stands out from today. Through this experience, I think you might be telling me...

_____

_____

_____

_____

_____

As I think about tomorrow, God, I pray that...

_____

_____

_____

_____

_____

_____

_____

_____ / _____ / _____

Thank you, God, for the gift of today. As I honestly review the events of the past 24 hours and pay attention to my feelings, I know your loving presence surrounds me. Bless my journal and our time spent together.

I felt alive in your presence today, God, when...

_____

_____

_____

_____

I struggled to feel your presence today, God, when...

_____

_____

_____

_____

God, I want to share more deeply with you about one moment that stands out from today. Through this experience, I think you might be telling me...

_____

_____

_____

_____

_____

As I think about tomorrow, God, I pray that...

_____

_____

_____

_____

_____

_____

_____ / _____ / _____

Thank you, God, for the gift of today. As I honestly review the events of the past 24 hours and pay attention to my feelings, I know your loving presence surrounds me. Bless my journal and our time spent together.

I felt alive in your presence today, God, when...

_____

_____

_____

_____

I struggled to feel your presence today, God, when...

_____

_____

_____

_____

God, I want to share more deeply with you about one moment that stands out from today. Through this experience, I think you might be telling me...

_____

_____

_____

_____

_____

As I think about tomorrow, God, I pray that...

_____

_____

_____

_____

_____

_____

_____ / _____ / _____

Thank you, God, for the gift of today. As I honestly review the events of the past 24 hours and pay attention to my feelings, I know your loving presence surrounds me. Bless my journal and our time spent together.

I felt alive in your presence today, God, when...

_____

_____

_____

_____

_____

I struggled to feel your presence today, God, when...

_____

_____

_____

_____

God, I want to share more deeply with you about one moment that stands out from today. Through this experience, I think you might be telling me...

_____

_____

_____

_____

_____

As I think about tomorrow, God, I pray that...

_____

_____

_____

_____

_____

_____

_____

_____/_____/_____

Thank you, God, for the gift of today. As I honestly review the events of the past 24 hours and pay attention to my feelings, I know your loving presence surrounds me. Bless my journal and our time spent together.

I felt alive in your presence today, God, when...

_____

_____

_____

_____

I struggled to feel your presence today, God, when...

_____

_____

_____

_____

God, I want to share more deeply with you about one moment that stands out from today. Through this experience, I think you might be telling me...

_____

_____

_____

_____

As I think about tomorrow, God, I pray that...

_____

_____

_____

_____

_____

_____

_____ / _____ / _____

Thank you, God, for the gift of today. As I honestly review the events of the past 24 hours and pay attention to my feelings, I know your loving presence surrounds me. Bless my journal and our time spent together.

I felt alive in your presence today, God, when...

_____

_____

_____

_____

I struggled to feel your presence today, God, when...

_____

_____

_____

_____

God, I want to share more deeply with you about one moment that stands out from today. Through this experience, I think you might be telling me...

_____

_____

_____

_____

_____

As I think about tomorrow, God, I pray that...

_____

_____

_____

_____

_____

_____

_____ / _____ / _____

Thank you, God, for the gift of today. As I honestly review the events of the past 24 hours and pay attention to my feelings, I know your loving presence surrounds me. Bless my journal and our time spent together.

I felt alive in your presence today, God, when...

_____

_____

_____

_____

I struggled to feel your presence today, God, when...

_____

_____

_____

_____

God, I want to share more deeply with you about one moment that stands out from today. Through this experience, I think you might be telling me...

_____

_____

_____

_____

_____

As I think about tomorrow, God, I pray that...

_____

_____

_____

_____

_____

_____

_____ / _____ / _____

Thank you, God, for the gift of today. As I honestly review the events of the past 24 hours and pay attention to my feelings, I know your loving presence surrounds me. Bless my journal and our time spent together.

I felt alive in your presence today, God, when...

_____

_____

_____

_____

I struggled to feel your presence today, God, when...

_____

_____

_____

God, I want to share more deeply with you about one moment that stands out from today. Through this experience, I think you might be telling me...

_____

_____

_____

_____

As I think about tomorrow, God, I pray that...

_____

_____

_____

_____

_____

_____

_____ / _____ / _____

Thank you, God, for the gift of today. As I honestly review the events of the past 24 hours and pay attention to my feelings, I know your loving presence surrounds me. Bless my journal and our time spent together.

I felt alive in your presence today, God, when...

_____

_____

_____

_____

_____

I struggled to feel your presence today, God, when...

_____

_____

_____

_____

God, I want to share more deeply with you about one moment that stands out from today. Through this experience, I think you might be telling me...

_____

_____

_____

_____

_____

As I think about tomorrow, God, I pray that...

_____

_____

_____

_____

_____

_____

_____/_____/_____

Thank you, God, for the gift of today. As I honestly review the events of the past 24 hours and pay attention to my feelings, I know your loving presence surrounds me. Bless my journal and our time spent together.

I felt alive in your presence today, God, when...

_____

_____

_____

_____

_____

I struggled to feel your presence today, God, when...

_____

_____

_____

_____

God, I want to share more deeply with you about one moment that stands out from today. Through this experience, I think you might be telling me...

_____

_____

_____

_____

_____

As I think about tomorrow, God, I pray that...

_____

_____

_____

_____

_____

_____

_____ / _____ / _____

Thank you, God, for the gift of today. As I honestly review the events of the past 24 hours and pay attention to my feelings, I know your loving presence surrounds me. Bless my journal and our time spent together.

I felt alive in your presence today, God, when...

_____

_____

_____

_____

I struggled to feel your presence today, God, when...

_____

_____

_____

_____

God, I want to share more deeply with you about one moment that stands out from today. Through this experience, I think you might be telling me...

_____

_____

_____

_____

_____

As I think about tomorrow, God, I pray that...

_____

_____

_____

_____

_____

_____

Thank you, God, for the gift of today. As I honestly review the events of the past 24 hours and pay attention to my feelings, I know your loving presence surrounds me. Bless my journal and our time spent together.

I felt alive in your presence today, God, when...

I struggled to feel your presence today, God, when...

God, I want to share more deeply with you about one moment that stands out from today. Through this experience, I think you might be telling me...

As I think about tomorrow, God, I pray that...

_____/_____/_____

Thank you, God, for the gift of today. As I honestly review the events of the past 24 hours and pay attention to my feelings, I know your loving presence surrounds me. Bless my journal and our time spent together.

I felt alive in your presence today, God, when...

_____
_____
_____
_____

I struggled to feel your presence today, God, when...

_____
_____
_____
_____

God, I want to share more deeply with you about one moment that stands out from today. Through this experience, I think you might be telling me...

_____
_____
_____
_____
_____

As I think about tomorrow, God, I pray that...

_____
_____
_____
_____
_____
_____

_____ / _____ / _____

Thank you, God, for the gift of today. As I honestly review the events of the past 24 hours and pay attention to my feelings, I know your loving presence surrounds me. Bless my journal and our time spent together.

I felt alive in your presence today, God, when...

_____

_____

_____

_____

I struggled to feel your presence today, God, when...

_____

_____

_____

_____

God, I want to share more deeply with you about one moment that stands out from today. Through this experience, I think you might be telling me...

_____

_____

_____

_____

As I think about tomorrow, God, I pray that...

_____

_____

_____

_____

_____

_____

_____ / _____ / _____

Thank you, God, for the gift of today. As I honestly review the events of the past 24 hours and pay attention to my feelings, I know your loving presence surrounds me. Bless my journal and our time spent together.

I felt alive in your presence today, God, when...

_____

_____

_____

_____

I struggled to feel your presence today, God, when...

_____

_____

_____

God, I want to share more deeply with you about one moment that stands out from today. Through this experience, I think you might be telling me...

_____

_____

_____

_____

As I think about tomorrow, God, I pray that...

_____

_____

_____

_____

_____

_____

_____ / _____ / _____

Thank you, God, for the gift of today. As I honestly review the events of the past 24 hours and pay attention to my feelings, I know your loving presence surrounds me. Bless my journal and our time spent together.

I felt alive in your presence today, God, when...

_____

_____

_____

_____

I struggled to feel your presence today, God, when...

_____

_____

_____

_____

God, I want to share more deeply with you about one moment that stands out from today. Through this experience, I think you might be telling me...

_____

_____

_____

_____

As I think about tomorrow, God, I pray that...

_____

_____

_____

_____

_____

_____

All the things in this world
are gifts of God,
created for us,
to be the means by which
we can come to know him better,
love him more surely,
and serve him more faithfully.

- St. Ignatius

_____ / _____ / _____

Thank you, God, for the gift of today. As I honestly review the events of the past 24 hours and pay attention to my feelings, I know your loving presence surrounds me. Bless my journal and our time spent together.

I felt alive in your presence today, God, when...

_____

_____

_____

_____

I struggled to feel your presence today, God, when...

_____

_____

_____

_____

God, I want to share more deeply with you about one moment that stands out from today. Through this experience, I think you might be telling me...

_____

_____

_____

_____

As I think about tomorrow, God, I pray that...

_____

_____

_____

_____

_____

_____

_____ / _____ / _____

Thank you, God, for the gift of today. As I honestly review the events of the past 24 hours and pay attention to my feelings, I know your loving presence surrounds me. Bless my journal and our time spent together.

I felt alive in your presence today, God, when...

_____

_____

_____

_____

_____

I struggled to feel your presence today, God, when...

_____

_____

_____

_____

God, I want to share more deeply with you about one moment that stands out from today. Through this experience, I think you might be telling me...

_____

_____

_____

_____

_____

As I think about tomorrow, God, I pray that...

_____

_____

_____

_____

_____

_____

_____ / _____ / _____

Thank you, God, for the gift of today. As I honestly review the events of the past 24 hours and pay attention to my feelings, I know your loving presence surrounds me. Bless my journal and our time spent together.

I felt alive in your presence today, God, when...

_____

_____

_____

_____

I struggled to feel your presence today, God, when...

_____

_____

_____

God, I want to share more deeply with you about one moment that stands out from today. Through this experience, I think you might be telling me...

_____

_____

_____

_____

As I think about tomorrow, God, I pray that...

_____

_____

_____

_____

_____

_____

_____ / _____ / _____

Thank you, God, for the gift of today. As I honestly review the events of the past 24 hours and pay attention to my feelings, I know your loving presence surrounds me. Bless my journal and our time spent together.

I felt alive in your presence today, God, when...

_____

_____

_____

_____

I struggled to feel your presence today, God, when...

_____

_____

_____

_____

God, I want to share more deeply with you about one moment that stands out from today. Through this experience, I think you might be telling me...

_____

_____

_____

_____

_____

As I think about tomorrow, God, I pray that...

_____

_____

_____

_____

_____

_____

_____ / _____ /

Thank you, God, for the gift of today. As I honestly review the events of the past 24 hours and pay attention to my feelings, I know your loving presence surrounds me. Bless my journal and our time spent together.

I felt alive in your presence today, God, when...

_____

_____

_____

_____

_____

I struggled to feel your presence today, God, when...

_____

_____

_____

_____

_____

God, I want to share more deeply with you about one moment that stands out from today. Through this experience, I think you might be telling me...

_____

_____

_____

_____

_____

As I think about tomorrow, God, I pray that...

_____

_____

_____

_____

_____

_____

_____

Thank you, God, for the gift of today. As I honestly review the events of the past 24 hours and pay attention to my feelings, I know your loving presence surrounds me. Bless my journal and our time spent together.

I felt alive in your presence today, God, when...

_____

_____

_____

_____

I struggled to feel your presence today, God, when...

_____

_____

_____

_____

God, I want to share more deeply with you about one moment that stands out from today. Through this experience, I think you might be telling me...

_____

_____

_____

_____

_____

As I think about tomorrow, God, I pray that...

_____

_____

_____

_____

_____

_____

_____ / _____ / _____

Thank you, God, for the gift of today. As I honestly review the events of the past 24 hours and pay attention to my feelings, I know your loving presence surrounds me. Bless my journal and our time spent together.

I felt alive in your presence today, God, when...

_____

_____

_____

_____

I struggled to feel your presence today, God, when...

_____

_____

_____

God, I want to share more deeply with you about one moment that stands out from today. Through this experience, I think you might be telling me...

_____

_____

_____

_____

As I think about tomorrow, God, I pray that...

_____

_____

_____

_____

_____

_____

Thank you, God, for the gift of today. As I honestly review the events of the past 24 hours and pay attention to my feelings, I know your loving presence surrounds me. Bless my journal and our time spent together.

I felt alive in your presence today, God, when...

_____

_____

_____

_____

_____

I struggled to feel your presence today, God, when...

_____

_____

_____

_____

God, I want to share more deeply with you about one moment that stands out from today. Through this experience, I think you might be telling me...

_____

_____

_____

_____

_____

As I think about tomorrow, God, I pray that...

_____

_____

_____

_____

_____

_____

_____/_____/_____

Thank you, God, for the gift of today. As I honestly review the events of the past 24 hours and pay attention to my feelings, I know your loving presence surrounds me. Bless my journal and our time spent together.

I felt alive in your presence today, God, when...

I struggled to feel your presence today, God, when...

God, I want to share more deeply with you about one moment that stands out from today. Through this experience, I think you might be telling me...

As I think about tomorrow, God, I pray that...

_____ / _____ / _____

Thank you, God, for the gift of today. As I honestly review the events of the past 24 hours and pay attention to my feelings, I know your loving presence surrounds me. Bless my journal and our time spent together.

I felt alive in your presence today, God, when...

_____

_____

_____

_____

_____

I struggled to feel your presence today, God, when...

_____

_____

_____

_____

_____

God, I want to share more deeply with you about one moment that stands out from today. Through this experience, I think you might be telling me...

_____

_____

_____

_____

_____

As I think about tomorrow, God, I pray that...

_____

_____

_____

_____

_____

_____

_____

Thank you, God, for the gift of today. As I honestly review the events of the past 24 hours and pay attention to my feelings, I know your loving presence surrounds me. Bless my journal and our time spent together.

I felt alive in your presence today, God, when...

_____

_____

_____

_____

I struggled to feel your presence today, God, when...

_____

_____

_____

_____

God, I want to share more deeply with you about one moment that stands out from today. Through this experience, I think you might be telling me...

_____

_____

_____

_____

As I think about tomorrow, God, I pray that...

_____

_____

_____

_____

_____

_____ / _____ / _____

Thank you, God, for the gift of today. As I honestly review the events of the past 24 hours and pay attention to my feelings, I know your loving presence surrounds me. Bless my journal and our time spent together.

I felt alive in your presence today, God, when...

_____

_____

_____

_____

I struggled to feel your presence today, God, when...

_____

_____

_____

_____

God, I want to share more deeply with you about one moment that stands out from today. Through this experience, I think you might be telling me...

_____

_____

_____

_____

As I think about tomorrow, God, I pray that...

_____

_____

_____

_____

_____

_____

_____ / _____ / _____

Thank you, God, for the gift of today. As I honestly review the events of the past 24 hours and pay attention to my feelings, I know your loving presence surrounds me. Bless my journal and our time spent together.

I felt alive in your presence today, God, when...

_____

_____

_____

_____

I struggled to feel your presence today, God, when...

_____

_____

_____

_____

God, I want to share more deeply with you about one moment that stands out from today. Through this experience, I think you might be telling me...

_____

_____

_____

_____

_____

As I think about tomorrow, God, I pray that...

_____

_____

_____

_____

_____

_____

_____ / _____ / _____

Thank you, God, for the gift of today. As I honestly review the events of the past 24 hours and pay attention to my feelings, I know your loving presence surrounds me. Bless my journal and our time spent together.

I felt alive in your presence today, God, when...

_____

_____

_____

_____

I struggled to feel your presence today, God, when...

_____

_____

_____

_____

God, I want to share more deeply with you about one moment that stands out from today. Through this experience, I think you might be telling me...

_____

_____

_____

_____

_____

As I think about tomorrow, God, I pray that...

_____

_____

_____

_____

_____

_____

_____

_____ / _____ / _____

Thank you, God, for the gift of today. As I honestly review the events of the past 24 hours and pay attention to my feelings, I know your loving presence surrounds me. Bless my journal and our time spent together.

I felt alive in your presence today, God, when...

_____

_____

_____

_____

_____

I struggled to feel your presence today, God, when...

_____

_____

_____

_____

God, I want to share more deeply with you about one moment that stands out from today. Through this experience, I think you might be telling me...

_____

_____

_____

_____

_____

As I think about tomorrow, God, I pray that...

_____

_____

_____

_____

_____

_____

_____ / _____ /

Thank you, God, for the gift of today. As I honestly review the events of the past 24 hours and pay attention to my feelings, I know your loving presence surrounds me. Bless my journal and our time spent together.

I felt alive in your presence today, God, when...

_____

_____

_____

_____

_____

I struggled to feel your presence today, God, when...

_____

_____

_____

_____

_____

God, I want to share more deeply with you about one moment that stands out from today. Through this experience, I think you might be telling me...

_____

_____

_____

_____

_____

_____

As I think about tomorrow, God, I pray that...

_____

_____

_____

_____

_____

_____

_____

Thank you, God, for the gift of today. As I honestly review the events of the past 24 hours and pay attention to my feelings, I know your loving presence surrounds me. Bless my journal and our time spent together.

I felt alive in your presence today, God, when...

_____

_____

_____

_____

I struggled to feel your presence today, God, when...

_____

_____

_____

_____

God, I want to share more deeply with you about one moment that stands out from today. Through this experience, I think you might be telling me...

_____

_____

_____

_____

_____

As I think about tomorrow, God, I pray that...

_____

_____

_____

_____

_____

_____

_____ / _____ / _____

Thank you, God, for the gift of today. As I honestly review the events of the past 24 hours and pay attention to my feelings, I know your loving presence surrounds me. Bless my journal and our time spent together.

I felt alive in your presence today, God, when...

_____

_____

_____

_____

I struggled to feel your presence today, God, when...

_____

_____

_____

God, I want to share more deeply with you about one moment that stands out from today. Through this experience, I think you might be telling me...

_____

_____

_____

_____

As I think about tomorrow, God, I pray that...

_____

_____

_____

_____

_____

_____

_____ / _____ / _____

Thank you, God, for the gift of today. As I honestly review the events of the past 24 hours and pay attention to my feelings, I know your loving presence surrounds me. Bless my journal and our time spent together.

I felt alive in your presence today, God, when...

_____

_____

_____

_____

I struggled to feel your presence today, God, when...

_____

_____

_____

God, I want to share more deeply with you about one moment that stands out from today. Through this experience, I think you might be telling me...

_____

_____

_____

_____

As I think about tomorrow, God, I pray that...

_____

_____

_____

_____

_____

_____

_____ / _____ / _____

Thank you, God, for the gift of today. As I honestly review the events of the past 24 hours and pay attention to my feelings, I know your loving presence surrounds me. Bless my journal and our time spent together.

I felt alive in your presence today, God, when...

_____

_____

_____

_____

I struggled to feel your presence today, God, when...

_____

_____

_____

_____

God, I want to share more deeply with you about one moment that stands out from today. Through this experience, I think you might be telling me...

_____

_____

_____

_____

_____

As I think about tomorrow, God, I pray that...

_____

_____

_____

_____

_____

_____

_____ / _____ / _____

Thank you, God, for the gift of today. As I honestly review the events of the past 24 hours and pay attention to my feelings, I know your loving presence surrounds me. Bless my journal and our time spent together.

I felt alive in your presence today, God, when...

_____

_____

_____

_____

I struggled to feel your presence today, God, when...

_____

_____

_____

God, I want to share more deeply with you about one moment that stands out from today. Through this experience, I think you might be telling me...

_____

_____

_____

_____

As I think about tomorrow, God, I pray that...

_____

_____

_____

_____

_____

_____

_____ / _____ / _____

Thank you, God, for the gift of today. As I honestly review the events of the past 24 hours and pay attention to my feelings, I know your loving presence surrounds me. Bless my journal and our time spent together.

I felt alive in your presence today, God, when...

_____

_____

_____

_____

I struggled to feel your presence today, God, when...

_____

_____

_____

_____

God, I want to share more deeply with you about one moment that stands out from today. Through this experience, I think you might be telling me...

_____

_____

_____

_____

_____

As I think about tomorrow, God, I pray that...

_____

_____

_____

_____

_____

_____

Thank you, God, for the gift of today. As I honestly review the events of the past 24 hours and pay attention to my feelings, I know your loving presence surrounds me. Bless my journal and our time spent together.

I felt alive in your presence today, God, when...

_____

_____

_____

_____

I struggled to feel your presence today, God, when...

_____

_____

_____

_____

God, I want to share more deeply with you about one moment that stands out from today. Through this experience, I think you might be telling me...

_____

_____

_____

_____

_____

As I think about tomorrow, God, I pray that...

_____

_____

_____

_____

_____

_____

_____ / _____ / _____

Thank you, God, for the gift of today. As I honestly review the events of the past 24 hours and pay attention to my feelings, I know your loving presence surrounds me. Bless my journal and our time spent together.

I felt alive in your presence today, God, when...

I struggled to feel your presence today, God, when...

God, I want to share more deeply with you about one moment that stands out from today. Through this experience, I think you might be telling me...

As I think about tomorrow, God, I pray that...

_____ / _____ / _____

Thank you, God, for the gift of today. As I honestly review the events of the past 24 hours and pay attention to my feelings, I know your loving presence surrounds me. Bless my journal and our time spent together.

I felt alive in your presence today, God, when...

_____

_____

_____

_____

_____

I struggled to feel your presence today, God, when...

_____

_____

_____

_____

_____

God, I want to share more deeply with you about one moment that stands out from today. Through this experience, I think you might be telling me...

_____

_____

_____

_____

_____

As I think about tomorrow, God, I pray that...

_____

_____

_____

_____

_____

_____

_____

_____ / _____ / _____

Thank you, God, for the gift of today. As I honestly review the events of the past 24 hours and pay attention to my feelings, I know your loving presence surrounds me. Bless my journal and our time spent together.

I felt alive in your presence today, God, when...

_____

_____

_____

_____

_____

I struggled to feel your presence today, God, when...

_____

_____

_____

_____

God, I want to share more deeply with you about one moment that stands out from today. Through this experience, I think you might be telling me...

_____

_____

_____

_____

_____

As I think about tomorrow, God, I pray that...

_____

_____

_____

_____

_____

_____

Thank you, God, for the gift of today. As I honestly review the events of the past 24 hours and pay attention to my feelings, I know your loving presence surrounds me. Bless my journal and our time spent together.

I felt alive in your presence today, God, when...

_____

_____

_____

_____

I struggled to feel your presence today, God, when...

_____

_____

_____

_____

God, I want to share more deeply with you about one moment that stands out from today. Through this experience, I think you might be telling me...

_____

_____

_____

_____

_____

As I think about tomorrow, God, I pray that...

_____

_____

_____

_____

_____

_____

_____/_____/_____

Thank you, God, for the gift of today. As I honestly review the events of the past 24 hours and pay attention to my feelings, I know your loving presence surrounds me. Bless my journal and our time spent together.

I felt alive in your presence today, God, when...

_____

_____

_____

_____

I struggled to feel your presence today, God, when...

_____

_____

_____

God, I want to share more deeply with you about one moment that stands out from today. Through this experience, I think you might be telling me...

_____

_____

_____

_____

As I think about tomorrow, God, I pray that...

_____

_____

_____

_____

_____

_____

_____ / _____ / _____

Thank you, God, for the gift of today. As I honestly review the events of the past 24 hours and pay attention to my feelings, I know your loving presence surrounds me. Bless my journal and our time spent together.

I felt alive in your presence today, God, when...

....
....
....
....

I struggled to feel your presence today, God, when...

....
....
....
....

God, I want to share more deeply with you about one moment that stands out from today. Through this experience, I think you might be telling me...

....
....
....
....

As I think about tomorrow, God, I pray that...

....
....
....
....
....
....

_____ / _____ / _____

Thank you, God, for the gift of today. As I honestly review the events of the past 24 hours and pay attention to my feelings, I know your loving presence surrounds me. Bless my journal and our time spent together.

I felt alive in your presence today, God, when...

_____
_____
_____
_____
_____

I struggled to feel your presence today, God, when...

_____
_____
_____
_____

God, I want to share more deeply with you about one moment that stands out from today. Through this experience, I think you might be telling me...

_____
_____
_____
_____
_____

As I think about tomorrow, God, I pray that...

_____
_____
_____
_____
_____
_____
_____

_____ / _____ / _____

Thank you, God, for the gift of today. As I honestly review the events of the past 24 hours and pay attention to my feelings, I know your loving presence surrounds me. Bless my journal and our time spent together.

I felt alive in your presence today, God, when...

_____

_____

_____

_____

I struggled to feel your presence today, God, when...

_____

_____

_____

_____

God, I want to share more deeply with you about one moment that stands out from today. Through this experience, I think you might be telling me...

_____

_____

_____

_____

_____

As I think about tomorrow, God, I pray that...

_____

_____

_____

_____

_____

_____

_____

ad majorem

dei gloriam

FOR THE GREATER GLORY OF GOD

- St. Ignatius

Thank you, God, for the gift of today. As I honestly review the events of the past 24 hours and pay attention to my feelings, I know your loving presence surrounds me. Bless my journal and our time spent together.

I felt alive in your presence today, God, when...

_____

_____

_____

_____

I struggled to feel your presence today, God, when...

_____

_____

_____

_____

God, I want to share more deeply with you about one moment that stands out from today. Through this experience, I think you might be telling me...

_____

_____

_____

_____

_____

As I think about tomorrow, God, I pray that...

_____

_____

_____

_____

_____

_____

_____ / _____ / _____

Thank you, God, for the gift of today. As I honestly review the events of the past 24 hours and pay attention to my feelings, I know your loving presence surrounds me. Bless my journal and our time spent together.

I felt alive in your presence today, God, when...

_____
_____
_____
_____

I struggled to feel your presence today, God, when...

_____
_____
_____
_____

God, I want to share more deeply with you about one moment that stands out from today. Through this experience, I think you might be telling me...

_____
_____
_____
_____
_____

As I think about tomorrow, God, I pray that...

_____
_____
_____
_____
_____
_____

_____ / _____ /

Thank you, God, for the gift of today. As I honestly review the events of the past 24 hours and pay attention to my feelings, I know your loving presence surrounds me. Bless my journal and our time spent together.

I felt alive in your presence today, God, when...

_____

_____

_____

_____

_____

I struggled to feel your presence today, God, when...

_____

_____

_____

_____

God, I want to share more deeply with you about one moment that stands out from today. Through this experience, I think you might be telling me...

_____

_____

_____

_____

_____

As I think about tomorrow, God, I pray that...

_____

_____

_____

_____

_____

_____

_____ / _____ / _____

Thank you, God, for the gift of today. As I honestly review the events of the past 24 hours and pay attention to my feelings, I know your loving presence surrounds me. Bless my journal and our time spent together.

I felt alive in your presence today, God, when...

_____

_____

_____

_____

I struggled to feel your presence today, God, when...

_____

_____

_____

_____

God, I want to share more deeply with you about one moment that stands out from today. Through this experience, I think you might be telling me...

_____

_____

_____

_____

As I think about tomorrow, God, I pray that...

_____

_____

_____

_____

_____

_____

_____ / _____ /

Thank you, God, for the gift of today. As I honestly review the events of the past 24 hours and pay attention to my feelings, I know your loving presence surrounds me. Bless my journal and our time spent together.

I felt alive in your presence today, God, when...

_____

_____

_____

_____

I struggled to feel your presence today, God, when...

_____

_____

_____

_____

God, I want to share more deeply with you about one moment that stands out from today. Through this experience, I think you might be telling me...

_____

_____

_____

_____

As I think about tomorrow, God, I pray that...

_____

_____

_____

_____

_____

_____

_____/_____/_____

Thank you, God, for the gift of today. As I honestly review the events of the past 24 hours and pay attention to my feelings, I know your loving presence surrounds me. Bless my journal and our time spent together.

I felt alive in your presence today, God, when...

_____

_____

_____

_____

_____

I struggled to feel your presence today, God, when...

_____

_____

_____

_____

God, I want to share more deeply with you about one moment that stands out from today. Through this experience, I think you might be telling me...

_____

_____

_____

_____

_____

As I think about tomorrow, God, I pray that...

_____

_____

_____

_____

_____

_____

_____

_____ / _____ / _____

Thank you, God, for the gift of today. As I honestly review the events of the past 24 hours and pay attention to my feelings, I know your loving presence surrounds me. Bless my journal and our time spent together.

I felt alive in your presence today, God, when...

_____

_____

_____

_____

I struggled to feel your presence today, God, when...

_____

_____

_____

_____

God, I want to share more deeply with you about one moment that stands out from today. Through this experience, I think you might be telling me...

_____

_____

_____

_____

_____

As I think about tomorrow, God, I pray that...

_____

_____

_____

_____

_____

_____

_____ / _____ / _____

Thank you, God, for the gift of today. As I honestly review the events of the past 24 hours and pay attention to my feelings, I know your loving presence surrounds me. Bless my journal and our time spent together.

I felt alive in your presence today, God, when...

_____

_____

_____

_____

_____

I struggled to feel your presence today, God, when...

_____

_____

_____

_____

God, I want to share more deeply with you about one moment that stands out from today. Through this experience, I think you might be telling me...

_____

_____

_____

_____

_____

As I think about tomorrow, God, I pray that...

_____

_____

_____

_____

_____

_____

_____

_____ / _____ / _____

Thank you, God, for the gift of today. As I honestly review the events of the past 24 hours and pay attention to my feelings, I know your loving presence surrounds me. Bless my journal and our time spent together.

I felt alive in your presence today, God, when...

_____

_____

_____

_____

I struggled to feel your presence today, God, when...

_____

_____

_____

_____

God, I want to share more deeply with you about one moment that stands out from today. Through this experience, I think you might be telling me...

_____

_____

_____

_____

_____

As I think about tomorrow, God, I pray that...

_____

_____

_____

_____

_____

_____

_____ / _____ /

Thank you, God, for the gift of today. As I honestly review the events of the past 24 hours and pay attention to my feelings, I know your loving presence surrounds me. Bless my journal and our time spent together.

I felt alive in your presence today, God, when...

_____

_____

_____

_____

I struggled to feel your presence today, God, when...

_____

_____

_____

_____

God, I want to share more deeply with you about one moment that stands out from today. Through this experience, I think you might be telling me...

_____

_____

_____

_____

_____

As I think about tomorrow, God, I pray that...

_____

_____

_____

_____

_____

_____

_____

_____ / _____ / _____

Thank you, God, for the gift of today. As I honestly review the events of the past 24 hours and pay attention to my feelings, I know your loving presence surrounds me. Bless my journal and our time spent together.

I felt alive in your presence today, God, when...

_____

_____

_____

_____

I struggled to feel your presence today, God, when...

_____

_____

_____

_____

God, I want to share more deeply with you about one moment that stands out from today. Through this experience, I think you might be telling me...

_____

_____

_____

_____

_____

As I think about tomorrow, God, I pray that...

_____

_____

_____

_____

_____

_____

_____ / _____ /

Thank you, God, for the gift of today. As I honestly review the events of the past 24 hours and pay attention to my feelings, I know your loving presence surrounds me. Bless my journal and our time spent together.

I felt alive in your presence today, God, when...

_____

_____

_____

_____

I struggled to feel your presence today, God, when...

_____

_____

_____

God, I want to share more deeply with you about one moment that stands out from today. Through this experience, I think you might be telling me...

_____

_____

_____

_____

_____

As I think about tomorrow, God, I pray that...

_____

_____

_____

_____

_____

_____

Thank you, God, for the gift of today. As I honestly review the events of the past 24 hours and pay attention to my feelings, I know your loving presence surrounds me. Bless my journal and our time spent together.

I felt alive in your presence today, God, when...

_____

_____

_____

_____

I struggled to feel your presence today, God, when...

_____

_____

_____

_____

God, I want to share more deeply with you about one moment that stands out from today. Through this experience, I think you might be telling me...

_____

_____

_____

_____

_____

As I think about tomorrow, God, I pray that...

_____

_____

_____

_____

_____

_____

_____ / _____ / _____

Thank you, God, for the gift of today. As I honestly review the events of the past 24 hours and pay attention to my feelings, I know your loving presence surrounds me. Bless my journal and our time spent together.

I felt alive in your presence today, God, when...

_____

_____

_____

_____

I struggled to feel your presence today, God, when...

_____

_____

_____

_____

God, I want to share more deeply with you about one moment that stands out from today. Through this experience, I think you might be telling me...

_____

_____

_____

_____

As I think about tomorrow, God, I pray that...

_____

_____

_____

_____

_____

_____

Thank you, God, for the gift of today. As I honestly review the events of the past 24 hours and pay attention to my feelings, I know your loving presence surrounds me. Bless my journal and our time spent together.

I felt alive in your presence today, God, when...

_____

_____

_____

_____

I struggled to feel your presence today, God, when...

_____

_____

_____

_____

God, I want to share more deeply with you about one moment that stands out from today. Through this experience, I think you might be telling me...

_____

_____

_____

_____

_____

As I think about tomorrow, God, I pray that...

_____

_____

_____

_____

_____

_____

_____ / _____ /

Thank you, God, for the gift of today. As I honestly review the events of the past 24 hours and pay attention to my feelings, I know your loving presence surrounds me. Bless my journal and our time spent together.

I felt alive in your presence today, God, when...

_____
_____
_____
_____
_____

I struggled to feel your presence today, God, when...

_____
_____
_____
_____

God, I want to share more deeply with you about one moment that stands out from today. Through this experience, I think you might be telling me...

_____
_____
_____
_____
_____

As I think about tomorrow, God, I pray that...

_____
_____
_____
_____
_____
_____

_____ / _____ / _____

Thank you, God, for the gift of today. As I honestly review the events of the past 24 hours and pay attention to my feelings, I know your loving presence surrounds me. Bless my journal and our time spent together.

I felt alive in your presence today, God, when...

_____
_____
_____
_____
_____

I struggled to feel your presence today, God, when...

_____
_____
_____
_____
_____

God, I want to share more deeply with you about one moment that stands out from today. Through this experience, I think you might be telling me...

_____
_____
_____
_____
_____

As I think about tomorrow, God, I pray that...

_____
_____
_____
_____
_____
_____
_____

_____/_____/_____

Thank you, God, for the gift of today. As I honestly review the events of the past 24 hours and pay attention to my feelings, I know your loving presence surrounds me. Bless my journal and our time spent together.

I felt alive in your presence today, God, when...

_____

_____

_____

_____

_____

I struggled to feel your presence today, God, when...

_____

_____

_____

_____

God, I want to share more deeply with you about one moment that stands out from today. Through this experience, I think you might be telling me...

_____

_____

_____

_____

_____

As I think about tomorrow, God, I pray that...

_____

_____

_____

_____

_____

_____

_____ / _____ / _____

Thank you, God, for the gift of today. As I honestly review the events of the past 24 hours and pay attention to my feelings, I know your loving presence surrounds me. Bless my journal and our time spent together.

I felt alive in your presence today, God, when...

_____

_____

_____

_____

I struggled to feel your presence today, God, when...

_____

_____

_____

_____

God, I want to share more deeply with you about one moment that stands out from today. Through this experience, I think you might be telling me...

_____

_____

_____

_____

As I think about tomorrow, God, I pray that...

_____

_____

_____

_____

_____

_____

_____ / _____ /

Thank you, God, for the gift of today. As I honestly review the events of the past 24 hours and pay attention to my feelings, I know your loving presence surrounds me. Bless my journal and our time spent together.

I felt alive in your presence today, God, when...

I struggled to feel your presence today, God, when...

God, I want to share more deeply with you about one moment that stands out from today. Through this experience, I think you might be telling me...

As I think about tomorrow, God, I pray that...

_____ / _____ / _____

Thank you, God, for the gift of today. As I honestly review the events of the past 24 hours and pay attention to my feelings, I know your loving presence surrounds me. Bless my journal and our time spent together.

I felt alive in your presence today, God, when...

_____

_____

_____

_____

I struggled to feel your presence today, God, when...

_____

_____

_____

_____

God, I want to share more deeply with you about one moment that stands out from today. Through this experience, I think you might be telling me...

_____

_____

_____

_____

_____

As I think about tomorrow, God, I pray that...

_____

_____

_____

_____

_____

_____

_____ / _____ / _____

Thank you, God, for the gift of today. As I honestly review the events of the past 24 hours and pay attention to my feelings, I know your loving presence surrounds me. Bless my journal and our time spent together.

I felt alive in your presence today, God, when...

_____

_____

_____

_____

_____

I struggled to feel your presence today, God, when...

_____

_____

_____

_____

God, I want to share more deeply with you about one moment that stands out from today. Through this experience, I think you might be telling me...

_____

_____

_____

_____

_____

As I think about tomorrow, God, I pray that...

_____

_____

_____

_____

_____

_____

_____ / _____ /

Thank you, God, for the gift of today. As I honestly review the events of the past 24 hours and pay attention to my feelings, I know your loving presence surrounds me. Bless my journal and our time spent together.

I felt alive in your presence today, God, when...

_____

_____

_____

_____

I struggled to feel your presence today, God, when...

_____

_____

_____

_____

God, I want to share more deeply with you about one moment that stands out from today. Through this experience, I think you might be telling me...

_____

_____

_____

_____

_____

As I think about tomorrow, God, I pray that...

_____

_____

_____

_____

_____

_____

_____ / _____ /

Thank you, God, for the gift of today. As I honestly review the events of the past 24 hours and pay attention to my feelings, I know your loving presence surrounds me. Bless my journal and our time spent together.

I felt alive in your presence today, God, when...

I struggled to feel your presence today, God, when...

God, I want to share more deeply with you about one moment that stands out from today. Through this experience, I think you might be telling me...

As I think about tomorrow, God, I pray that...

Thank you, God, for the gift of today. As I honestly review the events of the past 24 hours and pay attention to my feelings, I know your loving presence surrounds me. Bless my journal and our time spent together.

I felt alive in your presence today, God, when...

_____

_____

_____

_____

I struggled to feel your presence today, God, when...

_____

_____

_____

_____

God, I want to share more deeply with you about one moment that stands out from today. Through this experience, I think you might be telling me...

_____

_____

_____

_____

As I think about tomorrow, God, I pray that...

_____

_____

_____

_____

_____

_____

_____ / _____ / _____

Thank you, God, for the gift of today. As I honestly review the events of the past 24 hours and pay attention to my feelings, I know your loving presence surrounds me. Bless my journal and our time spent together.

I felt alive in your presence today, God, when...

_____

_____

_____

_____

I struggled to feel your presence today, God, when...

_____

_____

_____

_____

God, I want to share more deeply with you about one moment that stands out from today. Through this experience, I think you might be telling me...

_____

_____

_____

_____

_____

As I think about tomorrow, God, I pray that...

_____

_____

_____

_____

_____

_____

_____/_____/_____

Thank you, God, for the gift of today. As I honestly review the events of the past 24 hours and pay attention to my feelings, I know your loving presence surrounds me. Bless my journal and our time spent together.

I felt alive in your presence today, God, when...

_____

_____

_____

_____

_____

I struggled to feel your presence today, God, when...

_____

_____

_____

_____

God, I want to share more deeply with you about one moment that stands out from today. Through this experience, I think you might be telling me...

_____

_____

_____

_____

_____

As I think about tomorrow, God, I pray that...

_____

_____

_____

_____

_____

_____

_____ / _____ / _____

Thank you, God, for the gift of today. As I honestly review the events of the past 24 hours and pay attention to my feelings, I know your loving presence surrounds me. Bless my journal and our time spent together.

I felt alive in your presence today, God, when...

_____

_____

_____

_____

I struggled to feel your presence today, God, when...

_____

_____

_____

God, I want to share more deeply with you about one moment that stands out from today. Through this experience, I think you might be telling me...

_____

_____

_____

_____

As I think about tomorrow, God, I pray that...

_____

_____

_____

_____

_____

_____

_____ / _____ /

Thank you, God, for the gift of today. As I honestly review the events of the past 24 hours and pay attention to my feelings, I know your loving presence surrounds me. Bless my journal and our time spent together.

I felt alive in your presence today, God, when...

_____

_____

_____

_____

I struggled to feel your presence today, God, when...

_____

_____

_____

God, I want to share more deeply with you about one moment that stands out from today. Through this experience, I think you might be telling me...

_____

_____

_____

_____

As I think about tomorrow, God, I pray that...

_____

_____

_____

_____

_____

_____

_____ / _____ /

Thank you, God, for the gift of today. As I honestly review the events of the past 24 hours and pay attention to my feelings, I know your loving presence surrounds me. Bless my journal and our time spent together.

I felt alive in your presence today, God, when...

_____

_____

_____

_____

I struggled to feel your presence today, God, when...

_____

_____

_____

_____

God, I want to share more deeply with you about one moment that stands out from today. Through this experience, I think you might be telling me...

_____

_____

_____

_____

_____

As I think about tomorrow, God, I pray that...

_____

_____

_____

_____

_____

_____

_____ / _____ /

Thank you, God, for the gift of today. As I honestly review the events of the past 24 hours and pay attention to my feelings, I know your loving presence surrounds me. Bless my journal and our time spent together.

I felt alive in your presence today, God, when...

I struggled to feel your presence today, God, when...

God, I want to share more deeply with you about one moment that stands out from today. Through this experience, I think you might be telling me...

As I think about tomorrow, God, I pray that...

Love
is shown
more in deeds
than in words.

- St. Ignatius

Thank you, God, for the gift of today. As I honestly review the events of the past 24 hours and pay attention to my feelings, I know your loving presence surrounds me. Bless my journal and our time spent together.

I felt alive in your presence today, God, when...

_____

_____

_____

_____

I struggled to feel your presence today, God, when...

_____

_____

_____

_____

God, I want to share more deeply with you about one moment that stands out from today. Through this experience, I think you might be telling me...

_____

_____

_____

_____

As I think about tomorrow, God, I pray that...

_____

_____

_____

_____

_____

_____

_____ / _____ / _____

Thank you, God, for the gift of today. As I honestly review the events of the past 24 hours and pay attention to my feelings, I know your loving presence surrounds me. Bless my journal and our time spent together.

I felt alive in your presence today, God, when...

_____
_____
_____
_____

I struggled to feel your presence today, God, when...

_____
_____
_____
_____

God, I want to share more deeply with you about one moment that stands out from today. Through this experience, I think you might be telling me...

_____
_____
_____
_____

As I think about tomorrow, God, I pray that...

_____
_____
_____
_____
_____

_____/_____/_____

Thank you, God, for the gift of today. As I honestly review the events of the past 24 hours and pay attention to my feelings, I know your loving presence surrounds me. Bless my journal and our time spent together.

I felt alive in your presence today, God, when...

_____

_____

_____

_____

_____

I struggled to feel your presence today, God, when...

_____

_____

_____

_____

God, I want to share more deeply with you about one moment that stands out from today. Through this experience, I think you might be telling me...

_____

_____

_____

_____

As I think about tomorrow, God, I pray that...

_____

_____

_____

_____

_____

_____

_____ / _____ / _____

Thank you, God, for the gift of today. As I honestly review the events of the past 24 hours and pay attention to my feelings, I know your loving presence surrounds me. Bless my journal and our time spent together.

I felt alive in your presence today, God, when...

_____

_____

_____

_____

_____

I struggled to feel your presence today, God, when...

_____

_____

_____

_____

God, I want to share more deeply with you about one moment that stands out from today. Through this experience, I think you might be telling me...

_____

_____

_____

_____

_____

As I think about tomorrow, God, I pray that...

_____

_____

_____

_____

_____

_____

_____

_____ / _____ / _____

Thank you, God, for the gift of today. As I honestly review the events of the past 24 hours and pay attention to my feelings, I know your loving presence surrounds me. Bless my journal and our time spent together.

I felt alive in your presence today, God, when...

_____

_____

_____

_____

I struggled to feel your presence today, God, when...

_____

_____

_____

_____

God, I want to share more deeply with you about one moment that stands out from today. Through this experience, I think you might be telling me...

_____

_____

_____

_____

As I think about tomorrow, God, I pray that...

_____

_____

_____

_____

_____

_____

Thank you, God, for the gift of today. As I honestly review the events of the past 24 hours and pay attention to my feelings, I know your loving presence surrounds me. Bless my journal and our time spent together.

I felt alive in your presence today, God, when...

I struggled to feel your presence today, God, when...

God, I want to share more deeply with you about one moment that stands out from today. Through this experience, I think you might be telling me...

As I think about tomorrow, God, I pray that...

Thank you, God, for the gift of today. As I honestly review the events of the past 24 hours and pay attention to my feelings, I know your loving presence surrounds me. Bless my journal and our time spent together.

I felt alive in your presence today, God, when...

_____

_____

_____

_____

_____

I struggled to feel your presence today, God, when...

_____

_____

_____

_____

God, I want to share more deeply with you about one moment that stands out from today. Through this experience, I think you might be telling me...

_____

_____

_____

_____

As I think about tomorrow, God, I pray that...

_____

_____

_____

_____

_____

_____

_____ / _____ /

Thank you, God, for the gift of today. As I honestly review the events of the past 24 hours and pay attention to my feelings, I know your loving presence surrounds me. Bless my journal and our time spent together.

I felt alive in your presence today, God, when...

_____

_____

_____

_____

I struggled to feel your presence today, God, when...

_____

_____

_____

_____

God, I want to share more deeply with you about one moment that stands out from today. Through this experience, I think you might be telling me...

_____

_____

_____

_____

_____

As I think about tomorrow, God, I pray that...

_____

_____

_____

_____

_____

_____

Thank you, God, for the gift of today. As I honestly review the events of the past 24 hours and pay attention to my feelings, I know your loving presence surrounds me. Bless my journal and our time spent together.

I felt alive in your presence today, God, when...

_____

_____

_____

_____

I struggled to feel your presence today, God, when...

_____

_____

_____

_____

God, I want to share more deeply with you about one moment that stands out from today. Through this experience, I think you might be telling me...

_____

_____

_____

_____

_____

As I think about tomorrow, God, I pray that...

_____

_____

_____

_____

_____

_____

_____ / _____ / _____

Thank you, God, for the gift of today. As I honestly review the events of the past 24 hours and pay attention to my feelings, I know your loving presence surrounds me. Bless my journal and our time spent together.

I felt alive in your presence today, God, when...

I struggled to feel your presence today, God, when...

God, I want to share more deeply with you about one moment that stands out from today. Through this experience, I think you might be telling me...

As I think about tomorrow, God, I pray that...

_____ / _____ / _____

Thank you, God, for the gift of today. As I honestly review the events of the past 24 hours and pay attention to my feelings, I know your loving presence surrounds me. Bless my journal and our time spent together.

I felt alive in your presence today, God, when...

_____

_____

_____

_____

_____

I struggled to feel your presence today, God, when...

_____

_____

_____

_____

God, I want to share more deeply with you about one moment that stands out from today. Through this experience, I think you might be telling me...

_____

_____

_____

_____

_____

As I think about tomorrow, God, I pray that...

_____

_____

_____

_____

_____

_____

_____/_____/_____

Thank you, God, for the gift of today. As I honestly review the events of the past 24 hours and pay attention to my feelings, I know your loving presence surrounds me. Bless my journal and our time spent together.

I felt alive in your presence today, God, when...

_____

_____

_____

_____

I struggled to feel your presence today, God, when...

_____

_____

_____

_____

God, I want to share more deeply with you about one moment that stands out from today. Through this experience, I think you might be telling me...

_____

_____

_____

_____

_____

As I think about tomorrow, God, I pray that...

_____

_____

_____

_____

_____

_____

_____ / _____ / _____

Thank you, God, for the gift of today. As I honestly review the events of the past 24 hours and pay attention to my feelings, I know your loving presence surrounds me. Bless my journal and our time spent together.

I felt alive in your presence today, God, when...

_____
_____
_____
_____
_____

I struggled to feel your presence today, God, when...

_____
_____
_____
_____
_____

God, I want to share more deeply with you about one moment that stands out from today. Through this experience, I think you might be telling me...

_____
_____
_____
_____
_____

As I think about tomorrow, God, I pray that...

_____
_____
_____
_____
_____
_____

_____ / _____ / _____

Thank you, God, for the gift of today. As I honestly review the events of the past 24 hours and pay attention to my feelings, I know your loving presence surrounds me. Bless my journal and our time spent together.

I felt alive in your presence today, God, when...

_____

_____

_____

_____

I struggled to feel your presence today, God, when...

_____

_____

_____

_____

God, I want to share more deeply with you about one moment that stands out from today. Through this experience, I think you might be telling me...

_____

_____

_____

_____

_____

As I think about tomorrow, God, I pray that...

_____

_____

_____

_____

_____

_____

_____ / _____ / _____

Thank you, God, for the gift of today. As I honestly review the events of the past 24 hours and pay attention to my feelings, I know your loving presence surrounds me. Bless my journal and our time spent together.

I felt alive in your presence today, God, when...

_____
_____
_____
_____

I struggled to feel your presence today, God, when...

_____
_____
_____
_____

God, I want to share more deeply with you about one moment that stands out from today. Through this experience, I think you might be telling me...

_____
_____
_____
_____
_____

As I think about tomorrow, God, I pray that...

_____
_____
_____
_____
_____
_____

_____/_____/_____

Thank you, God, for the gift of today. As I honestly review the events of the past 24 hours and pay attention to my feelings, I know your loving presence surrounds me. Bless my journal and our time spent together.

I felt alive in your presence today, God, when...

_____

_____

_____

_____

I struggled to feel your presence today, God, when...

_____

_____

_____

_____

God, I want to share more deeply with you about one moment that stands out from today. Through this experience, I think you might be telling me...

_____

_____

_____

_____

_____

As I think about tomorrow, God, I pray that...

_____

_____

_____

_____

_____

_____

_____ / _____ / _____

Thank you, God, for the gift of today. As I honestly review the events of the past 24 hours and pay attention to my feelings, I know your loving presence surrounds me. Bless my journal and our time spent together.

I felt alive in your presence today, God, when...

_____

_____

_____

_____

I struggled to feel your presence today, God, when...

_____

_____

_____

_____

God, I want to share more deeply with you about one moment that stands out from today. Through this experience, I think you might be telling me...

_____

_____

_____

_____

_____

As I think about tomorrow, God, I pray that...

_____

_____

_____

_____

_____

_____

Thank you, God, for the gift of today. As I honestly review the events of the past 24 hours and pay attention to my feelings, I know your loving presence surrounds me. Bless my journal and our time spent together.

I felt alive in your presence today, God, when...

_____

_____

_____

_____

I struggled to feel your presence today, God, when...

_____

_____

_____

_____

God, I want to share more deeply with you about one moment that stands out from today. Through this experience, I think you might be telling me...

_____

_____

_____

_____

_____

As I think about tomorrow, God, I pray that...

_____

_____

_____

_____

_____

_____

_____ / _____ / _____

Thank you, God, for the gift of today. As I honestly review the events of the past 24 hours and pay attention to my feelings, I know your loving presence surrounds me. Bless my journal and our time spent together.

I felt alive in your presence today, God, when...

_____

_____

_____

_____

I struggled to feel your presence today, God, when...

_____

_____

_____

_____

God, I want to share more deeply with you about one moment that stands out from today. Through this experience, I think you might be telling me...

_____

_____

_____

_____

As I think about tomorrow, God, I pray that...

_____

_____

_____

_____

_____

_____

_____ / _____ / _____

Thank you, God, for the gift of today. As I honestly review the events of the past 24 hours and pay attention to my feelings, I know your loving presence surrounds me. Bless my journal and our time spent together.

I felt alive in your presence today, God, when...

_____

_____

_____

_____

_____

I struggled to feel your presence today, God, when...

_____

_____

_____

_____

God, I want to share more deeply with you about one moment that stands out from today. Through this experience, I think you might be telling me...

_____

_____

_____

_____

_____

As I think about tomorrow, God, I pray that...

_____

_____

_____

_____

_____

_____

_____ / _____ / _____

Thank you, God, for the gift of today. As I honestly review the events of the past 24 hours and pay attention to my feelings, I know your loving presence surrounds me. Bless my journal and our time spent together.

I felt alive in your presence today, God, when...

_____
_____
_____
_____
_____

I struggled to feel your presence today, God, when...

_____
_____
_____
_____

God, I want to share more deeply with you about one moment that stands out from today. Through this experience, I think you might be telling me...

_____
_____
_____
_____
_____

As I think about tomorrow, God, I pray that...

_____
_____
_____
_____
_____
_____

_____/_____/_____

Thank you, God, for the gift of today. As I honestly review the events of the past 24 hours and pay attention to my feelings, I know your loving presence surrounds me. Bless my journal and our time spent together.

I felt alive in your presence today, God, when...

_____

_____

_____

_____

I struggled to feel your presence today, God, when...

_____

_____

_____

_____

God, I want to share more deeply with you about one moment that stands out from today. Through this experience, I think you might be telling me...

_____

_____

_____

_____

_____

As I think about tomorrow, God, I pray that...

_____

_____

_____

_____

_____

_____

_____/_____/_____

Thank you, God, for the gift of today. As I honestly review the events of the past 24 hours and pay attention to my feelings, I know your loving presence surrounds me. Bless my journal and our time spent together.

I felt alive in your presence today, God, when...

_____

_____

_____

_____

I struggled to feel your presence today, God, when...

_____

_____

_____

_____

God, I want to share more deeply with you about one moment that stands out from today. Through this experience, I think you might be telling me...

_____

_____

_____

_____

As I think about tomorrow, God, I pray that...

_____

_____

_____

_____

_____

_____

_____ / _____ /

Thank you, God, for the gift of today. As I honestly review the events of the past 24 hours and pay attention to my feelings, I know your loving presence surrounds me. Bless my journal and our time spent together.

I felt alive in your presence today, God, when...

_____

_____

_____

_____

I struggled to feel your presence today, God, when...

_____

_____

_____

_____

God, I want to share more deeply with you about one moment that stands out from today. Through this experience, I think you might be telling me...

_____

_____

_____

_____

_____

As I think about tomorrow, God, I pray that...

_____

_____

_____

_____

_____

_____

_____ / _____ / _____

Thank you, God, for the gift of today. As I honestly review the events of the past 24 hours and pay attention to my feelings, I know your loving presence surrounds me. Bless my journal and our time spent together.

I felt alive in your presence today, God, when...

_____

_____

_____

_____

_____

I struggled to feel your presence today, God, when...

_____

_____

_____

_____

God, I want to share more deeply with you about one moment that stands out from today. Through this experience, I think you might be telling me...

_____

_____

_____

_____

_____

As I think about tomorrow, God, I pray that...

_____

_____

_____

_____

_____

_____

_____

_____ / _____ / _____

Thank you, God, for the gift of today. As I honestly review the events of the past 24 hours and pay attention to my feelings, I know your loving presence surrounds me. Bless my journal and our time spent together.

I felt alive in your presence today, God, when...

_____

_____

_____

_____

I struggled to feel your presence today, God, when...

_____

_____

_____

God, I want to share more deeply with you about one moment that stands out from today. Through this experience, I think you might be telling me...

_____

_____

_____

_____

As I think about tomorrow, God, I pray that...

_____

_____

_____

_____

_____

_____

_____ / _____ /

Thank you, God, for the gift of today. As I honestly review the events of the past 24 hours and pay attention to my feelings, I know your loving presence surrounds me. Bless my journal and our time spent together.

I felt alive in your presence today, God, when...

_____

_____

_____

_____

I struggled to feel your presence today, God, when...

_____

_____

_____

_____

God, I want to share more deeply with you about one moment that stands out from today. Through this experience, I think you might be telling me...

_____

_____

_____

_____

As I think about tomorrow, God, I pray that...

_____

_____

_____

_____

_____

_____

Thank you, God, for the gift of today. As I honestly review the events of the past 24 hours and pay attention to my feelings, I know your loving presence surrounds me. Bless my journal and our time spent together.

I felt alive in your presence today, God, when...

I struggled to feel your presence today, God, when...

God, I want to share more deeply with you about one moment that stands out from today. Through this experience, I think you might be telling me...

As I think about tomorrow, God, I pray that...

Thank you, God, for the gift of today. As I honestly review the events of the past 24 hours and pay attention to my feelings, I know your loving presence surrounds me. Bless my journal and our time spent together.

I felt alive in your presence today, God, when...

_____

_____

_____

_____

I struggled to feel your presence today, God, when...

_____

_____

_____

_____

God, I want to share more deeply with you about one moment that stands out from today. Through this experience, I think you might be telling me...

_____

_____

_____

_____

As I think about tomorrow, God, I pray that...

_____

_____

_____

_____

_____

_____

_____ / _____ /

Thank you, God, for the gift of today. As I honestly review the events of the past 24 hours and pay attention to my feelings, I know your loving presence surrounds me. Bless my journal and our time spent together.

I felt alive in your presence today, God, when...

_____

_____

_____

_____

I struggled to feel your presence today, God, when...

_____

_____

_____

God, I want to share more deeply with you about one moment that stands out from today. Through this experience, I think you might be telling me...

_____

_____

_____

_____

As I think about tomorrow, God, I pray that...

_____

_____

_____

_____

_____

Thank you, God, for the gift of today. As I honestly review the events of the past 24 hours and pay attention to my feelings, I know your loving presence surrounds me. Bless my journal and our time spent together.

I felt alive in your presence today, God, when...

_____

_____

_____

_____

I struggled to feel your presence today, God, when...

_____

_____

_____

_____

God, I want to share more deeply with you about one moment that stands out from today. Through this experience, I think you might be telling me...

_____

_____

_____

_____

_____

As I think about tomorrow, God, I pray that...

_____

_____

_____

_____

_____

_____

TAKE, LORD,
AND
RECEIVE
ALL MY LIBERTY,
MY MEMORY,
MY UNDERSTANDING
AND MY ENTIRE WILL,
ALL I HAVE AND CALL MY OWN.

YOU HAVE GIVEN
ALL TO ME.
TO YOU, LORD, I RETURN IT.

EVERYTHING IS YOURS;
DO WITH IT WHAT YOU WILL.
GIVE ME ONLY YOUR LOVE
AND YOUR GRACE.
THAT IS ENOUGH FOR ME.

- ST. IGNATIUS

_____/_____/_____

Thank you, God, for the gift of today. As I honestly review the events of the past 24 hours and pay attention to my feelings, I know your loving presence surrounds me. Bless my journal and our time spent together.

I felt alive in your presence today, God, when...

_____

_____

_____

_____

I struggled to feel your presence today, God, when...

_____

_____

_____

_____

God, I want to share more deeply with you about one moment that stands out from today. Through this experience, I think you might be telling me...

_____

_____

_____

_____

As I think about tomorrow, God, I pray that...

_____

_____

_____

_____

_____

_____

_____ / _____ / _____

Thank you, God, for the gift of today. As I honestly review the events of the past 24 hours and pay attention to my feelings, I know your loving presence surrounds me. Bless my journal and our time spent together.

I felt alive in your presence today, God, when...

_____

_____

_____

_____

I struggled to feel your presence today, God, when...

_____

_____

_____

_____

God, I want to share more deeply with you about one moment that stands out from today. Through this experience, I think you might be telling me...

_____

_____

_____

_____

_____

As I think about tomorrow, God, I pray that...

_____

_____

_____

_____

_____

_____

_____ / _____ /

Thank you, God, for the gift of today. As I honestly review the events of the past 24 hours and pay attention to my feelings, I know your loving presence surrounds me. Bless my journal and our time spent together.

I felt alive in your presence today, God, when...

_____

_____

_____

_____

_____

I struggled to feel your presence today, God, when...

_____

_____

_____

_____

_____

God, I want to share more deeply with you about one moment that stands out from today. Through this experience, I think you might be telling me...

_____

_____

_____

_____

_____

As I think about tomorrow, God, I pray that...

_____

_____

_____

_____

_____

_____

_____ / _____ /

Thank you, God, for the gift of today. As I honestly review the events of the past 24 hours and pay attention to my feelings, I know your loving presence surrounds me. Bless my journal and our time spent together.

I felt alive in your presence today, God, when...

_____

_____

_____

_____

I struggled to feel your presence today, God, when...

_____

_____

_____

God, I want to share more deeply with you about one moment that stands out from today. Through this experience, I think you might be telling me...

_____

_____

_____

_____

As I think about tomorrow, God, I pray that...

_____

_____

_____

_____

_____

Thank you, God, for the gift of today. As I honestly review the events of the past 24 hours and pay attention to my feelings, I know your loving presence surrounds me. Bless my journal and our time spent together.

I felt alive in your presence today, God, when...

_____

_____

_____

_____

I struggled to feel your presence today, God, when...

_____

_____

_____

God, I want to share more deeply with you about one moment that stands out from today. Through this experience, I think you might be telling me...

_____

_____

_____

_____

As I think about tomorrow, God, I pray that...

_____

_____

_____

_____

_____

_____

_____/_____/_____

Thank you, God, for the gift of today. As I honestly review the events of the past 24 hours and pay attention to my feelings, I know your loving presence surrounds me. Bless my journal and our time spent together.

I felt alive in your presence today, God, when...

_____

_____

_____

_____

_____

I struggled to feel your presence today, God, when...

_____

_____

_____

_____

God, I want to share more deeply with you about one moment that stands out from today. Through this experience, I think you might be telling me...

_____

_____

_____

_____

_____

As I think about tomorrow, God, I pray that...

_____

_____

_____

_____

_____

_____

_____

_____ / _____ / _____

Thank you, God, for the gift of today. As I honestly review the events of the past 24 hours and pay attention to my feelings, I know your loving presence surrounds me. Bless my journal and our time spent together.

I felt alive in your presence today, God, when...

_____

_____

_____

_____

_____

I struggled to feel your presence today, God, when...

_____

_____

_____

_____

God, I want to share more deeply with you about one moment that stands out from today. Through this experience, I think you might be telling me...

_____

_____

_____

_____

_____

As I think about tomorrow, God, I pray that...

_____

_____

_____

_____

_____

_____

_____ / _____ / _____

Thank you, God, for the gift of today. As I honestly review the events of the past 24 hours and pay attention to my feelings, I know your loving presence surrounds me. Bless my journal and our time spent together.

I felt alive in your presence today, God, when...

_____
_____
_____
_____

I struggled to feel your presence today, God, when...

_____
_____
_____
_____

God, I want to share more deeply with you about one moment that stands out from today. Through this experience, I think you might be telling me...

_____
_____
_____
_____
_____

As I think about tomorrow, God, I pray that...

_____
_____
_____
_____
_____
_____

Thank you, God, for the gift of today. As I honestly review the events of the past 24 hours and pay attention to my feelings, I know your loving presence surrounds me. Bless my journal and our time spent together.

I felt alive in your presence today, God, when...

_____

_____

_____

_____

I struggled to feel your presence today, God, when...

_____

_____

_____

_____

God, I want to share more deeply with you about one moment that stands out from today. Through this experience, I think you might be telling me...

_____

_____

_____

_____

As I think about tomorrow, God, I pray that...

_____

_____

_____

_____

_____

_____

_____ / _____ / _____

Thank you, God, for the gift of today. As I honestly review the events of the past 24 hours and pay attention to my feelings, I know your loving presence surrounds me. Bless my journal and our time spent together.

I felt alive in your presence today, God, when...

_____
_____
_____
_____

I struggled to feel your presence today, God, when...

_____
_____
_____

God, I want to share more deeply with you about one moment that stands out from today. Through this experience, I think you might be telling me...

_____
_____
_____
_____
_____

As I think about tomorrow, God, I pray that...

_____
_____
_____
_____
_____
_____

_____ / _____ / _____

Thank you, God, for the gift of today. As I honestly review the events of the past 24 hours and pay attention to my feelings, I know your loving presence surrounds me. Bless my journal and our time spent together.

I felt alive in your presence today, God, when...

_____

_____

_____

_____

I struggled to feel your presence today, God, when...

_____

_____

_____

_____

God, I want to share more deeply with you about one moment that stands out from today. Through this experience, I think you might be telling me...

_____

_____

_____

_____

_____

As I think about tomorrow, God, I pray that...

_____

_____

_____

_____

_____

_____

_____ / _____ /

Thank you, God, for the gift of today. As I honestly review the events of the past 24 hours and pay attention to my feelings, I know your loving presence surrounds me. Bless my journal and our time spent together.

I felt alive in your presence today, God, when...

_____

_____

_____

_____

I struggled to feel your presence today, God, when...

_____

_____

_____

_____

God, I want to share more deeply with you about one moment that stands out from today. Through this experience, I think you might be telling me...

_____

_____

_____

_____

_____

As I think about tomorrow, God, I pray that...

_____

_____

_____

_____

_____

_____

_____ / _____ /

Thank you, God, for the gift of today. As I honestly review the events of the past 24 hours and pay attention to my feelings, I know your loving presence surrounds me. Bless my journal and our time spent together.

I felt alive in your presence today, God, when...

_____

_____

_____

_____

I struggled to feel your presence today, God, when...

_____

_____

_____

_____

God, I want to share more deeply with you about one moment that stands out from today. Through this experience, I think you might be telling me...

_____

_____

_____

_____

_____

As I think about tomorrow, God, I pray that...

_____

_____

_____

_____

_____

_____

_____ / _____ / _____

Thank you, God, for the gift of today. As I honestly review the events of the past 24 hours and pay attention to my feelings, I know your loving presence surrounds me. Bless my journal and our time spent together.

I felt alive in your presence today, God, when...

_____
_____
_____
_____

I struggled to feel your presence today, God, when...

_____
_____
_____
_____

God, I want to share more deeply with you about one moment that stands out from today. Through this experience, I think you might be telling me...

_____
_____
_____
_____
_____

As I think about tomorrow, God, I pray that...

_____
_____
_____
_____
_____
_____
_____

_____ / _____ / _____

Thank you, God, for the gift of today. As I honestly review the events of the past 24 hours and pay attention to my feelings, I know your loving presence surrounds me. Bless my journal and our time spent together.

I felt alive in your presence today, God, when...

_____
_____
_____
_____
_____

I struggled to feel your presence today, God, when...

_____
_____
_____
_____
_____

God, I want to share more deeply with you about one moment that stands out from today. Through this experience, I think you might be telling me...

_____
_____
_____
_____
_____

As I think about tomorrow, God, I pray that...

_____
_____
_____
_____
_____
_____
_____

Thank you, God, for the gift of today. As I honestly review the events of the past 24 hours and pay attention to my feelings, I know your loving presence surrounds me. Bless my journal and our time spent together.

I felt alive in your presence today, God, when...

_____

_____

_____

_____

I struggled to feel your presence today, God, when...

_____

_____

_____

_____

God, I want to share more deeply with you about one moment that stands out from today. Through this experience, I think you might be telling me...

_____

_____

_____

_____

_____

As I think about tomorrow, God, I pray that...

_____

_____

_____

_____

_____

_____

_____

_____ / _____ / _____

Thank you, God, for the gift of today. As I honestly review the events of the past 24 hours and pay attention to my feelings, I know your loving presence surrounds me. Bless my journal and our time spent together.

I felt alive in your presence today, God, when...

_____

_____

_____

_____

I struggled to feel your presence today, God, when...

_____

_____

_____

_____

God, I want to share more deeply with you about one moment that stands out from today. Through this experience, I think you might be telling me...

_____

_____

_____

_____

As I think about tomorrow, God, I pray that...

_____

_____

_____

_____

_____

_____

_____ / _____ /

Thank you, God, for the gift of today. As I honestly review the events of the past 24 hours and pay attention to my feelings, I know your loving presence surrounds me. Bless my journal and our time spent together.

I felt alive in your presence today, God, when...

_____

_____

_____

_____

_____

I struggled to feel your presence today, God, when...

_____

_____

_____

_____

God, I want to share more deeply with you about one moment that stands out from today. Through this experience, I think you might be telling me...

_____

_____

_____

_____

_____

As I think about tomorrow, God, I pray that...

_____

_____

_____

_____

_____

_____

_____

_____/_____/_____

Thank you, God, for the gift of today. As I honestly review the events of the past 24 hours and pay attention to my feelings, I know your loving presence surrounds me. Bless my journal and our time spent together.

I felt alive in your presence today, God, when...

_____

_____

_____

_____

I struggled to feel your presence today, God, when...

_____

_____

_____

_____

God, I want to share more deeply with you about one moment that stands out from today. Through this experience, I think you might be telling me...

_____

_____

_____

_____

As I think about tomorrow, God, I pray that...

_____

_____

_____

_____

_____

_____

_____ / _____ / _____

Thank you, God, for the gift of today. As I honestly review the events of the past 24 hours and pay attention to my feelings, I know your loving presence surrounds me. Bless my journal and our time spent together.

I felt alive in your presence today, God, when...

_____

_____

_____

_____

_____

I struggled to feel your presence today, God, when...

_____

_____

_____

_____

_____

God, I want to share more deeply with you about one moment that stands out from today. Through this experience, I think you might be telling me...

_____

_____

_____

_____

_____

_____

As I think about tomorrow, God, I pray that...

_____

_____

_____

_____

_____

_____

_____

_____ / _____ / _____

Thank you, God, for the gift of today. As I honestly review the events of the past 24 hours and pay attention to my feelings, I know your loving presence surrounds me. Bless my journal and our time spent together.

I felt alive in your presence today, God, when...

_____

_____

_____

_____

_____

I struggled to feel your presence today, God, when...

_____

_____

_____

_____

God, I want to share more deeply with you about one moment that stands out from today. Through this experience, I think you might be telling me...

_____

_____

_____

_____

_____

As I think about tomorrow, God, I pray that...

_____

_____

_____

_____

_____

_____

_____

_____/_____/_____

Thank you, God, for the gift of today. As I honestly review the events of the past 24 hours and pay attention to my feelings, I know your loving presence surrounds me. Bless my journal and our time spent together.

I felt alive in your presence today, God, when...

_____

_____

_____

_____

I struggled to feel your presence today, God, when...

_____

_____

_____

_____

God, I want to share more deeply with you about one moment that stands out from today. Through this experience, I think you might be telling me...

_____

_____

_____

_____

As I think about tomorrow, God, I pray that...

_____

_____

_____

_____

_____

_____

Go forth and set the world on

- St. Ignatius

some additional guidance

FOR PRAYING WITH YOUR JOURNAL

If you're new to the Examen or to prayer in general, you may be interested in some additional guidance. The Examen Journal's pages are formatted to reflect an approachable version of the five steps of the prayer described earlier.

Let's flesh out the page a bit. Feel free to come back to this if you're feeling stuck or if you need help unpacking your day.

Thank you, God, for the gift of today. As I honestly review the events of the past 24 hours and pay attention to my feelings, I know your loving presence surrounds me. Bless my journal and our time spent together.

Take a few moments to sit and be still. Turn off your computer. Silence your phone. Breathe.

If you have a favorite prayer that most connects you to God, pray that now.

Thank God for today...for all of its highs, for all of its lows, and for everything in between. Breathe.

Start to review your day. Begin with your first moments waking up. What was the first thing on your mind? As you move through the morning, afternoon, and evening...who did you see? Who did you eat with, converse with, work with? What happened? How did each experience make you feel?

Even the simplest of moments are important. God doesn't only show up in mountain top experiences. God is present in our everyday. Every emotion is meaningful.

I felt alive in your presence today, God, when...

When did you most feel God present today? When did you feel energized, joyful, or hopeful? When did you sense that God was working through you or through someone else? What beautiful people or experiences called to mind the image of God for you? When were you God to someone else?

I struggled to feel your presence today, God, when...

When did you least feel God present today? When did you feel angry, frustrated, or anxious? When did you feel despair? What voids were present in your heart today? Was there an experience for which you need to ask forgiveness?

God, I want to share more deeply with you about one moment that stands out from today. Through this experience, I think you might be telling me...

As you're reviewing the past 24 hours, try to focus on just one experience from the day. What emotions were most present in that moment? Recall to God what happened like you would confide in a close friend over a cup of coffee.

Be honest with yourself. Be free in your expression of emotion and your use of words.

What do you think God might be saying to you through that experience as well as this journaling time?

As I think about tomorrow, God, I pray that...

What would you like to ask of God for tomorrow? What gifts or graces do you need? Is there a relationship that needs healing? Is there an experience for which you need courage? What specifically in your life do you feel needs direction? Something else? Be specific. God hears even the quietest whispers of your heart.

Close your journaling time with a short prayer of your choosing thanking God for this time spent together.

connect

www.livetodaywellco.com
Instagram @livetodaywellco
facebook.com/livetodaywellco
#theexamenjournal